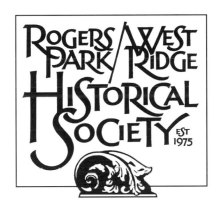

CHICAGO'S FAR NORTH SIDE

AN ILLUSTRATED HISTORY OF ROGERS PARK AND WEST RIDGE

NEAL SAMORS

MARY JO DOYLE

MARTIN LEWIN

MICHAEL WILLIAMS

ROGERS PARK/WEST RIDGE HISTORICAL SOCIETY

Published in the United States of America in 2000 by the Rogers Park/West Ridge Historical Society. Assistance provided by Chicago Historical Bookworks, Evanston IL 60202.

Edited by Neal Samors, Mary Jo Doyle, Sue Sosin, Marcee Williams and Marilou Kessler.

Produced by James B. Kirkpatrick in Century Schoolbook and Engravers Roman Bold using Adobe PageMaker 6.5.

Book Design by Michael Williams.

Printed by Great Lakes Graphics, Inc., Skokie Illinois.

ISBN:0-92447-231-X - soft cover
ISBN:0-92447-230-1 - hard cover

Cover: *Birch Forest at Lunt and Ashland, c. 1900*, photographer unknown.

Frontispiece: *Nortown Theatre, June 1956*, Theatre Historical Society of America, Elmhurst, IL; Photograph by Ray DeGoote, Jr.

For more information on the Rogers Park/West Ridge
   Historical Society, contact us at:
Phone: (773) 764-4078 or 4079
Fax: (773) 764-2824
Email: rpwrhs@aol.com
Web Site: www.rpwrhs.org.

CONTENTS

FOREWORD

KENAN HEISE

Behind every great collection or compilation, there is a persistent person. In this case, that of pulling together a visual history of Chicago's Rogers Park and West Ridge neighborhoods, that individual's name is Mary Jo Doyle, one of the founders of the local historical society.

To the residents of these two Far North Side communities, her identification is not news. Most of them, at least the long-time residents, have heard her repeat over the years the same question many times. It has been: Do you have any old photographs? We are especially looking for ones of the neighborhoods, families, houses, streets, religious institutions, schools, beaches or transportation.

This persistent questioning has paid off and made this book possible. Her neighbors have been most generous and shared with her and the Rogers Park/West Ridge Historical Society their pictures and the stories that go with them.

One of Mary Jo's favorites is the picture of the birch forest on the cover. In the late 1960s,

a high school student found it in the wall of her house when her father was doing some remodeling. She subsequently gave it to the historical society. Each picture has its explanation given to us along with the 250 cut-lines and photos in the book.

Just because the volume has now been published and the most interesting pictures printed, this does not mean the questioning will stop.

"There are a lot more photos out there, Doyle assures people. "I am certain of it."

The heart of the photo collection used in creating this book came from photographer Martin J. Schmidt who worked with the photos that were donated during his seventeen year tenure. He is past president of the Society, a man who has long been dedicated to the idea of preserving a visual history of Chicago and these two neighborhoods.

Chicago's Far North Side is a combined effort, the fruits of those neighbors and friends who have shared their photos and stories. More specifically, however, it is the work of its

Opposite: Peter Traes stands outside his Boots & Shoes shop at 4843 Clark (later 7048 N.) c. 1890.

authors and compilers, whose names appear on the title page. These include three individuals, in addition to Mary Jo Doyle, a life-long resident of the area.

Neal Samors, a native of Rogers Park and the principal writer for *Chicago's Far North Side*, is largely responsible for making this work a solid, readable and well-researched record of the two communities. His interest in the early days of his neighborhood began twenty years ago when he started looking into his family history and compiling reminiscences of Rogers Park. He found himself pulling this together in an article on the past of the community and then putting it into this book, making it a record of the area and its people.

Martin Lewin, a native of West Ridge and an active alumnus of Sullivan High School, wrote the material in the book, which covers the years 1946 through 1970. His detailed writing shows it was an era he experienced as well as researched.

Michael Williams came to Rogers Park from Barrington in 1984 to attend Loyola University. He is responsible for the exceptional design and graphics in the volume.

These four labored over this manuscript with love and a sense of mission for three years. They wanted to create more than a trivial record of their communities, not one that would merely interest the old timers and themselves. Their hope was a book, a history of their community, that would honor the blood, sweat, tears, joy and memories of those who have been the residents of Rogers Park and West Ridge since their inception as villages.

The two adjacent communities are multi-cultural, multi-racial and ethnically diverse neighborhoods. For more than one hundred years they have shown both stability and the willingness to change.

Their people, since the beginning, have been bonded by their love of the lake and its beaches, by their sense of being part of Chicago and their shared community institutions, churches, colleges and public and private schools. You can see this pride by walking their streets and talking with the residents. You can also perceive it in the photos that capture the past so well.

This is a most personal work, a photo album of two neighborhoods, full of the kind of pictures you might love to see pulled out at a picnic or the gathering of your extended family.

With it, we find ourselves looking back through the tunnel of time. If we are older, we say, "Yes, that's the way it looked." If we are younger or new to the neighborhood, we exclaim, "Oh, so that's how it was."

Chicago's Far North Side is a wonderful book to get lost in even if you have never set foot in the neighboring communities of Rogers Park or West Ridge. If you do, you just may find yourself there.

*Milk deliveryman Paul Einsweiler
poses on the steps of the J. F. Ure
Dairy wagon, c. 1914. The dairy was
located at 7527 N. Clark.*

INTRODUCTION

"Welcome to Rogers Park, Home of Loyola University Chicago." That's the sign greeting everyone who enters the Rogers Park community on Chicago's Far North Side at Devon, Sheridan and Broadway. It is one of the most famous locations in the neighborhood, since at one time or another during the last 165 years, Hayes Point, the St. Ignatius Church, the original Edgewater Golf Course, Loyola University, Mundelein College, and the Granada Theatre were situated at or near this intersection.

No sign is necessary to remind the hundreds of thousands of individuals that they have entered Rogers Park. This includes those who lived here from the turn of the century through the building boom of the 1920s and the worldwide Depression of the 1930s. Or individuals and families who resided in the neighborhood during World War II and the years immediately after that in the 1940s, the stable, yet changing 1950s, and the major political and social shifts of the 1960s. And, residents during Rogers Park's transitional years in the 1970s, 1980s and 1990s have their rec-ollections of life in the neighborhood. For those who spent their years in the neighborhood of Rogers Park, bounded by Lake Michigan on the east, Devon on the south, Ridge Avenue on the west and Howard Street on the north, there will always be a set of vivid memories.

The same range of memories would be true for those entering West Ridge. A ride on Ridge, shopping and dining on Devon, or passing Howard and Western would trigger recollections of life in West Ridge. Quite simply, there have always been many familiar sights in both Far North Side neighborhoods.

The experience of life in Rogers Park may have included eating at such diverse restaurants as Villa Girgenti, Papa Milano's, the Gold Coin, Allgauer's, the Town House, Ashkenaz or Cindy Sue's, or going to the movies at the Granada, the Adelphi, the 400, the Coed, the Howard or the Norshore. There may be recollections of attending services at a neighborhood church or synagogue, spending summers at the street-end beaches that stretch from

Opposite: Welcome sign at the intersection of Devon, Sheridan and Broadway, 2000.

Juneway Terrace all the way southward to Albion, or playing baseball, softball and football at Loyola, Pottawattomie or Touhy Parks.

There may also be memories of skating outdoors during the winter at Sam Leone's artificial rink; shopping on Howard, Morse, Jarvis, Sheridan, Devon or Clark; spending hours in the Rogers Park Library either on Greenleaf or Clark; or waiting for the elevated trains in the summer heat or winter snow to travel downtown from the Howard, Jarvis, Morse or Loyola stops. Memories may also include going to grammar school at St. Ignatius, St. Jerome, Field, Gale, Kilmer; attending high school at Sullivan; enrolling in college at Loyola University or Mundelein College; visiting the bars and nightclubs on Howard; riding the bus or elevated to shop in Evanston or going to Northwestern University football or Loyola basketball games.

While West Ridge is similar in many respects to Rogers Park, the population demographics have always been different and the housing now includes newer construction. To those who have called West Ridge their home (to some it will always be West Rogers Park), there will always be special memories about living, working, shopping and attending school in the neighborhood located west of the geological elevation, and remnant of the Ice Age, known as The Ridge.

Recollections might include: shopping on Devon; attending a religious institution; eating at the Black Angus, Randl's, Miller's, Pan Dee's, Kofield's, or the Pekin House; or seeing movies at the Nortown or the Cine. The remembrances might also include walking through Indian Boundary Park and feeding the animals in the little zoo; attending Armstrong, Boone, Clinton, Jamieson, Rogers, Stone, St. Hilary, St. Margaret Mary or St. Timothy; attending high school at Senn, Mather or St. Scholastica Academy, or going to baseball and softball games during summer evenings at Thillens Stadium. Residents of West Ridge can always visualize these and many other "snapshots".

The combination of shared memories creates a bond for current and former residents of Rogers Park and West Ridge. *Chicago's Far North Side, An Illustrated History of Rogers Park and West Ridge* has been written with all of you in mind. It is both the first comprehensive history of the communities and a compilation of the best photos that are available. The Rogers Park/West Ridge Historical Society, founded in 1975, has spent many years amassing what is clearly one of the broadest collections of neighborhood photographs to be found anywhere.

Members of the Society wanted to create a visual and narrative history of the neighborhoods from the earliest years when the first tavern was built on the Ridge in 1809; through the nineteenth century when Philip Rogers, his descendants and other early settlers built up the villages into neighborhoods; into a period of explosive growth and construction (first in the 1920s, and then after WW II); and until the present time when Rogers Park and West Ridge are among the most ethnically, racially and religiously diverse neighborhoods in the city of Chicago.

We hope that you find this book visually interesting and emotionally stimulating and that you learn new information about the rich histories of both neighborhoods. But, we especially hope the readers will decide to share this book with friends and family, and that it will reach many generations for years to come. One of the strong motivating forces for compiling a book such as this is that it can be fun for the reader. We hope that you enjoy this book.

Authors' Notes: A wide variety of sources were used in the preparation of this book, including interviews, personal records and public records, as well as newspapers, pamphlets, interviews documented by other sources, and journals and books. It is important to note that our review of these many sources sometimes revealed discrepancies and contradictions in historical information. We have sought to provide the reader with the most accurate information currently available about the people, places, dates, and events that have made up the histories of Rogers Park and West Ridge.

The terms, "community" and "neighborhood", have been used interchangeably throughout this book. However, Rogers Park and West Ridge are listed as two distinct areas in the seventy-seven Community Areas in the city of Chicago. These boundaries were created to gather statistics for the United States Census.

Chicago has also identified 176 neighborhoods in its delineation of areas of the city. In Chicago's neighborhood list, the names of East Rogers Park and West Rogers Park, as well as Nortown, are located within the Community Area boundaries of Rogers Park and West Ridge. Residents have often used a combination of this variety of designations in their discussions about the communities or neighborhoods on Chicago's Far North Side.

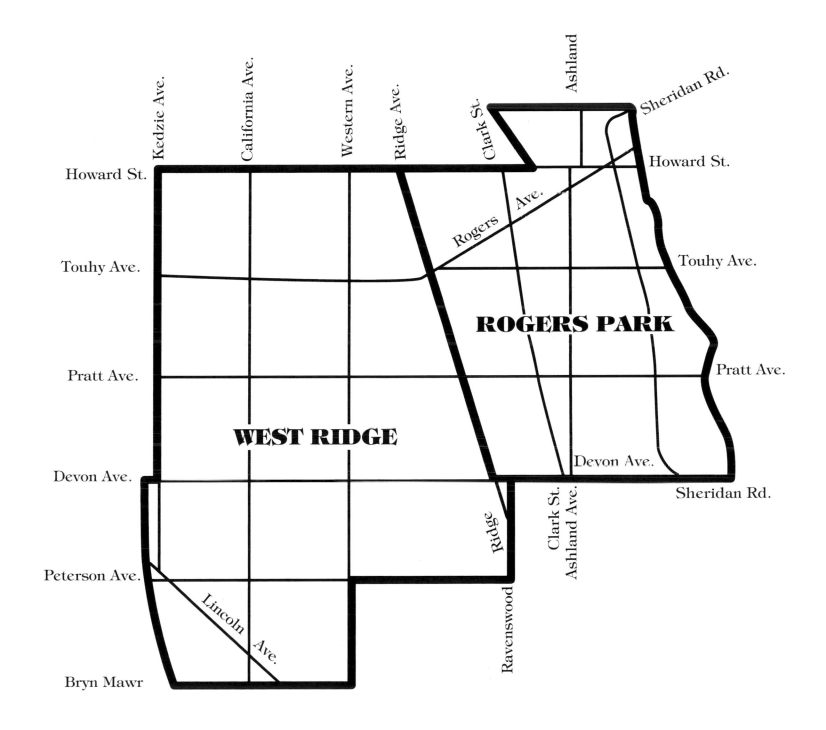

Years of Development
and Growth
1809 - 1893

Opposite: A view in 1875 of the east side of Clark, fifty feet south of Greenleaf, shows a row of two-story structures with business establishments on the first floor. The upper floor was usually occupied by the proprietor or a renter. The slope at the rear of the building indicates that it stood at the edge of one of the post-glacial beaches.

In the winter of 1834, twenty-two-year-old Philip McGregor Rogers and his brothers arrived in the Town of Chicago. They had come to America from County Louth, Ireland, and lived as children with their family in Watertown, a town in western New York near Lake Erie. The Northwest Territory was opened for settlement in the 1830s, and when they heard about the opportunities in the young town of Chicago at the southwest corner of Lake Michigan, the Rogers brothers decided to travel there. Their venture began in Sackets Harbor, New York, a port town at the end of the recently completed Erie Canal.

The brothers arrived in the Chicago area about the same time as three other Watertown residents who would have a significant influence on Chicago. They were William B. Ogden, Chicago's first mayor and the developer of the Galena and Chicago Union Railroad and the Chicago and Northwestern Railroad; John Calhoun, the founder and editor of Chicago's first newspaper; and Justin Butterfield, a leading member of the bar and a future federal land commissioner.

Apparently the Rogers brothers' initial reaction was less than positive, as they did not like Chicago's narrow, muddy streets and the town's icy, windy winter. Yet, with Lake Michigan frozen and impassable, Rogers and his brothers were forced to wait until spring before traveling west or returning to New York. But in the spring, Philip Rogers decided to remain in the region, although his brothers bought an ox team and went further west.

Soon after his decision to stay in the Chicago region, he married Mary Ward Masterson Hickey, widow of James Fox Hickey, who had extensive land holdings in the Sunnyside neighborhood, now a part of Edgewater. After initially purchasing farmland north and west of what would become Clark Street at Sunnyside Avenue, Philip Rogers moved further north to the Grosse Pointe District. In 1836 he bought the first

six hundred acres of an eventual total holding of sixteen hundred acres purchased from the U.S. government at the going rate of $1.25 an acre.

The land that Rogers bought was located above and below a ridge that had been shaped through a 300- to 400-million-years-old geological process. Lake Michigan and the waters of the Chicago River were formed as the last Ice Age retreated over 14,000 years, leaving behind a series of lakes, rivers, kettle moraines and beach ridges. Two of these ridges later became Ridge Boulevard and Clark Street.

The northern demarcation of the Rogers property was known as the Northern Indian Boundary Line. It received that designation as a result of the Treaty of 1816, signed in St. Louis between the United States government and the Sac and Fox tribes. In return for 50,000 acres of land provided by the U.S. government, the Native Americans ceded a strip of land starting from Lake Michigan, ten miles on either side of the Chicago River running southwest to the Kankakee, Illinois and Fox Rivers. The purpose of this cession was to move the Indian tribes out of the region as well as make it possible for the eventual construction of the Illinois and Michigan Canal connecting Chicago with the Mississippi River. The Southern Indian Boundary Line began at the mouth of the Calumet River, while the northern portion, an old Indian trail, began at Lake Michigan. That line would later become a road named Rogers Avenue, in the village, then neighborhood called Rogers Park, named in honor of Philip Rogers by his son-in-law, Patrick Leonard Touhy.

At that time (1834) the Indians used the swamps and rivers of the south side around what is now the Calumet district as their workshop. They fished, hunted, and trapped there. In the winter they took up their residence in the sheltered, wooded ridges along the north shore. Noticing this, Philip Rogers, my grandfather, decided to build his residence on the north side. It has always been the residence side of the city and always will be. **History of Rogers Park, Document #22, S. Rogers Touhy**

Opposite: The Lake Michigan shoreline at Lunt as seen around 1900.

Right: The Murphy farmhouse, on the former Indian Boundary Line, was located on the northwest corner of Rogers and Clark. Built in the 1840s, it was torn down in the 1930s.

Rogers constructed his home site on his new land approximately nine miles north of the Cook County courthouse. It was a simple, one-room log cabin near a stand of birch and maple trees along an elevated deer path known as the Ridge. The center of his property was located near the northeast corner of present day Lunt and Western Avenues. The Native Americans were the only residents of the area when Rogers arrived and he was the first white man to build a permanent structure there along the Ridge. There was an inn that served travelers, however, built around 1809, on the glacial ridge near the Rogers property. Riders used it while traveling the Frink and Walker stagecoach line between Chicago, Milwaukee and Green Bay on what had been a military road. Further north in Ridgeville, also known as the Grosse Pointe District, travelers could stop at the Baer or Mulford taverns along the Ridge for liquor, food or rest. In 1834, when Rogers settled there, some small Indian villages remained near the intersections of the Indian Boundary Line and Perry Street (now Rogers and Greenview Avenues) and the Indian Boundary Line and Clark Street.

When Mr. Rogers came west from Watertown, N.Y., it was prairie and woodland, trackless except for Indian trails and deer runs and a single road. The journey of nine miles to the courthouse in Chicago was perilous and tedious. **_Chicago Tribune, February 18, 1900_**

After building his cabin, Rogers laid out a farm, including a small apple orchard, planted cabbages and potatoes, and sold his vegetable crop to residents in the Town of Chicago. When Philip Rogers first started buying the land, it was covered with sand flats, scrub oaks and prairies with stands of timber. During the dry, hot summers, he could grow a crop of marsh grass for hay, but in normal years, the crop was worthless. Not much of the Roger's land was considered desirable, except for the wood used for charcoal, which was in great demand for use in cooking and heating. To make charcoal, Rogers needed workmen and the most skilled workers in this process were from Germany, so he employed German immigrants. After he abandoned the charcoal business, the German workers turned to farming.

Early Rogers Park Settlers

Philip Rogers used money from his successful truck farm business to buy additional land along, east and west of the Ridge. By the time of his death in 1856, he owned sixteen hundred acres south of the Northern Indian Boundary Line to Devon. After Rogers began to develop his land, other new settlers arrived in the region and purchased land along the Ridge. During the 1830s and 1840s, this group included: Edward Devlin, who purchased land north of Howard Street and east of the Ridge in 1841; Peter Smith, who bought 115 acres in 1840 along the Ridge from Pratt to Touhy and built a house at Farwell and the Ridge; Sarah Marshall, who, in 1844, purchased land for a farm at Jarvis and the Ridge; and Edward Murphy, who in 1840 bought land east of the Ridge and north of Rogers near the Clark Street tollgate.

Another settler, John O'Leary, arrived in Chicago in 1836 and bought forty acres for a farm in 1837 on Sunnyside, near Philip Rogers' initial land holdings. O'Leary lived there until 1840 when he bought 160 acres in Ridgeville that was north and east of Rogers' land. In 1850, O'Leary decided to go to California to seek his fortune in the Gold Rush, and returned in 1852 after some success. His grandson, David Philip O'Leary, reported that John had made more than $2,500. Then in 1859, he sold forty acres of his land that became Calvary Cemetery.

Sarah Marshall and her daughter, Ann, came to the area in 1842. She bought land near Philip Rogers after living on it for two years as a lessee. Initially, the Marshall house was a log cabin with the ground to the west cleared and cultivated by Native Americans before the Marshalls arrived. According to legend, Sarah Marshall prepared a chicken dinner for the engineers who were surveying the Ridge, and while dining, she convinced them to route the Ridge road around her property to bypass her cabin.

A second group of settlers, primarily from Luxembourg, moved into the region in the late 1840s and early 1850s. The Luxembourgers began immigrating to America around 1845, settling first in Wisconsin. In the spring of that year, Nicholas Kranz was one of the first Luxembourgers to come to the Chicago area. He built a log cabin at the northeast corner of Clark and Ridge, just south of Rogers Park. Then, in 1848, Nicholas Schreiber arrived in the area and purchased forty acres of land in Ridgeville. A few months after his death in 1853, Mrs. Schreiber had twin boys, Dominick and Michael. As the twins grew up, they joined their brother, John, in taking care of the farm. They also studied at the St. Henry parish school in the 1860s. The German immi-

The Joseph Ebert Tavern, shown in 1895, was situated at 3563 Ridge (later 6666 N.). The building included rooms to rent, a store and a tavern. Over the years, two famous restaurants, Allgauer's Fireside and Grassfield's on Ridge, were located on this site.

The Karthauser Inn was located at 3543 Ridge (later 6648 N.) with lodgings on the second floor and a beer garden to the south of the main building. The original inn was built in 1809 and was later a stagecoach stop.

grants, who had arrived earlier, intermarried with the Luxembourgers including the Zenders, Manns and Phillips, who had originally lived in the Rhein Province near Trier or Treves.

Peter Schmitt came here from Beirn-Trier in 1836. His daughter married John Zender, another early settler. Schmitt had 200 acres. He and Zender ran a saloon early. The first house was a blockhouse with a 10-foot stockade…The location of Schmitt's place is at 6665 Ridge Boulevard, but this is the third house that has been built. Peter Muno had a house one block south of Howard on Ridge that was built in 1842…In 1845, the land up here was described as having a little woodland, meadows and sloughs. **History of West Rogers Park, Document #2, Joseph Winandy**

In 1845 my father bought the Ridge Inn from Mr. Zender. It was a saloon and was built of logs. There were only five houses near the saloon and most of the trade was made up of people traveling to and from Chicago. Indians used to come into the old log house and ask for "firewater" and my father gave it to them out of the jug of whiskey. Ebert's Grove, which is next door to the Ridge Inn, opened a short time after my father started and was run by my brother. They didn't have names like Grove and Inn then, but were just called saloons. **History of Rogers Park, Document #34, Mrs. Karthauser**

Peter Muno came with Peter Phillip in 1842. When they arrived in the area Philip Rogers owned all of the land from Kedzie to Lake Michigan and from Pratt to Touhy. Muno was able to purchase forty acres of land north of Touhy, from Western to Kedzie, and Peter Phillip bought sixty acres to the north of Touhy from Ridge to Western.

By the time Peter Muno was established as a successful farmer he owned some eighty acres west of the "the Ridge". He had come over from Germany in 1842 with his wife and ten-year-old son, Henry, and had arrived in Chicago the same year, going out immediately to the country to become a homesteader. A patient and hard-working man, he built the house (7504 Ridge Avenue) and cleared his land and soon had most of it under cultivation. As the son grew older, he helped with the chores. During the first years that Peter Muno occupied the farmhouse the region was known as Ridgeville. It was formally organized as a township in 1850 under the same name and included a large part of what is today Evanston and what was formerly Lake View. A few years later Evanston and Lake View were organized into townships. Muno became the father of three more children, all girls. He continued farming (and) helped to found St. Henry's Roman Catholic Church at Ridge and Devon Avenue and he saw the coming of the North Western Railroad… **John Drury, <u>Old Chicago Houses</u>, 1941, pp. 207-208**

Rogers Park and West Ridge: 1850 to 1878

St. Henry, the first church built in the area, was constructed at the corner of Ridge and Devon in 1851. Built by Henry Fortmann, it was a small structure. It was replaced in 1871 with a larger building for $10,000. Across the street, on the southwest corner of Ridge and Devon, Angel Guardian Orphanage was opened in an old farmhouse in 1865. For many years, St. Henry was the only church between the City of Chicago boundary at Irving Park Road and Evanston (Ridgeville). The church membership consisted of Luxembourgers, Germans and Irish.

A group of Methodists had been seeking a location to build a new college north of the Indian Boundary and along the lake. In 1852, that group of businessmen and ministers received a charter for Northwestern University located in the town named for one of its founders, John Evans. Land for the school was purchased from Dr. Foster, and in 1855 the first building was completed and classes were held. At the same time, an amendment to the University charter was approved by the trustees that prohibited the sale of liquor within a four-mile radius around Northwestern. To the south of Evanston, this four-mile limit stretched to Devon Avenue and included the area that would become known as Rogers Park. This rule would have a significant effect on the separate development of Rogers Park and the section known as West Ridge.

In 1856, Philip Rogers died and the ownership of his sixteen hundred acres passed to his widow, his son, Philip Rogers, Jr., and his only daughter, Catherine. In 1865, following the Civil War, Catherine married Union Army Captain, Patrick Touhy. Touhy, an Irishman,

The Peter Muno house was built in the early 1840s at 4113 Ridge (later 7504 N.) and stood on this site for more than 120 years. Chicago Historical Society: ICHi-25904. Photograph by: J. Curtis Mitchell.

The original St. Henry Church, built in 1851, was located on the north side of Devon west of Ridge. This was the first Luxembourg Roman Catholic parish in Chicago. Chicago Historical Society photograph.

In 1871, Patrick and Catherine Touhy built the predominant home of the area, a 24-room mansion near the northeast corner of Chase Avenue and Clark Street at a cost of $18,000.

"Captain", as his friends familiarly called Patrick Leonard Touhy, and Mrs. Touhy built the historic homestead on North Clark Street near what is now Sherwin Avenue (sic). Many years later this fine mansion became the rendezvous of well known people from greater Chicago-among them Gen. Phil Sheridan, Gen. Sherman, Carter H. Harrison, Sr., Bishop DeKoven, and others. **North Shore News, October 11, 1945**

To defray the costs of the new mansion, Touhy sold a portion of his land holdings (225 acres) to a group of Evanston businessmen on September 10, 1872, and together they created the Rogers Park Land Company. They laid out a subdivision of forty-eight blocks adjacent to the original Touhy landsite bounded by Ridge, Ashland, Touhy and Pratt. The main section line was named after Patrick Touhy, and Catherine Touhy retained forty to fifty acres north of the new subdivision for their homestead. The east/west streets were named for several members of the Land Company: Paul and George Pratt, John V. Farwell, Luther L. Greenleaf, Stephen P. Lunt, George Estes, and Charles H. Morse. (Other members of the Company included Isaac R. Hitt and Andrew B. Jackson). The Land Company built sidewalks on Greenleaf from Clark to Paulina in 1873, as well as a small, twelve-inch tile sewer line on Touhy from Paulina to the Lake.

had been captured during the war, but was able to escape the infamous Confederate prison of Andersonville. Following the death of Philip Rogers, Jr. in 1869, his portion of the land went to his mother and sister. After Touhy and Catherine Rogers were married, he came into control of Catherine's land holdings of eight hundred acres. In 1869, Patrick Touhy platted a townsite, just east of the Chicago and Northwestern Railroad tracks that had been built in the 1850s, and named it Rogers Park after his late father-in-law.

The Land Company's agents sold lots and induced the purchasers to build on them. In order to improve the streets, take care of storm water, install sanitary sewerage and consider means of getting a supply of water for household use it was decided to incorporate under the state law and they did so. The place was changed from Township government to that of an incorporated village…With the incorporation of Rogers Park into a village there were some improvements made: the sale of intoxicating liquors was prohibited (under the four-mile rule), a village policeman was put on, also a volunteer fire company organized, contract was made with the Rogers Park Water Company to build a water plant, and surveys were made for sewerage. **History of Rogers Park, Document #28, Edward Sharp**

It was the Great Chicago Fire of 1871 and the need for new housing, as well as the completion of a route of the Chicago and Northwestern Railroad through Rogers Park in 1873, that had the greatest early impact on the development of the area. Chicago residents began to look for new locations to build their homes and the availability of transportation to and from the city made the village an attractive place to live.

Rogers Park's Incorporation

By 1874, there were fifty houses scattered in the small village of Rogers Park. Most were west of the train station at Greenleaf and Ravenswood, and the small business district on Clark between Lunt and Greenleaf. Because

of the Panic of 1873 and ensuing economic depression, the population in Rogers Park had a very slow growth. As a result, some of the original members of the Land Company withdrew their active participation. But, in April 1878, the village of Rogers Park was incorporated with its boundaries being Devon on the south, Ridge on the west, Rogers (Indian Boundary Line) on the north, and Lake Michigan on the east. As a result of the incorpora-

Patrick Touhy built this mansion, "The Oaks", for his wife, Catherine, daughter of Philip Rogers, first settler in Rogers Park. At one time a Potawatomi village occupied this land. The house, located at 5008 Clark (later 7339 N.), was torn down in 1917. This property exists today as a city park named for Mr. Touhy.

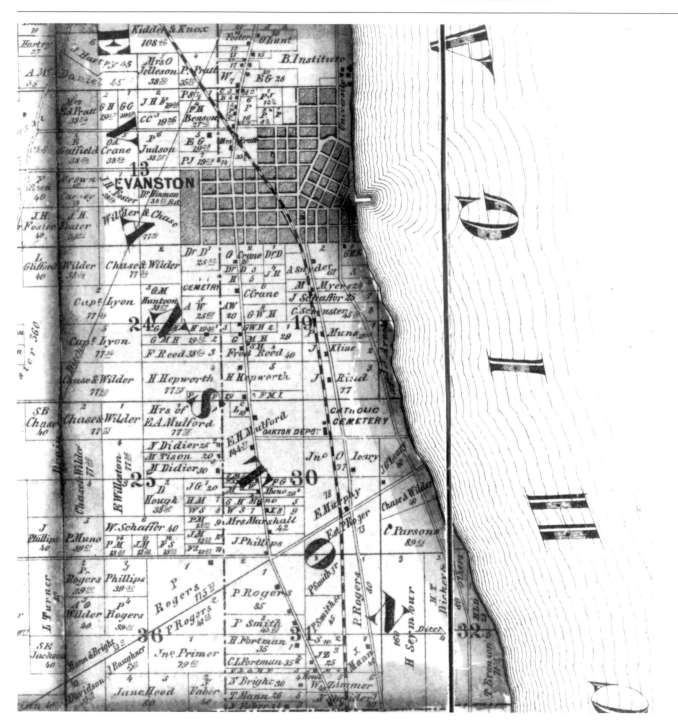

Left: The 1861 Flower Map showing portions of Rogers Park and West Ridge, indicating early property owners. Chicago Historical Society map.

Opposite top: A Clark Street scene in the late 1890s, between Lunt and Greenleaf, shows a small building on the left used as the office of Dr. W. D. Clark, 4816 Clark (later 7000 N. block). The two-story building on the right housed The Meat Market.

Opposite bottom: Mr. Franklin H. Doland, Callistus S. Ennis, Harlow W. Phelps and J. H. Daly were members of the Rogers Park Village Board in the 1890s.

tion, new investors joined the Rogers Park Land Company, including Cornelius Ceperly in 1872, and he would become one of Rogers Park's most important citizens, serving as village trustee, park commissioner and school board president.

Rogers Park at that time was considered the "sticks"... there were no lights, gas, sewerage and few sidewalks and you had to memorize the places where sidewalks ended so you wouldn't step into the mire. East of Ashland Boulevard was all swamp until the sewers were put in. In the spring the only dry spot in that district was on the northwest corner of Touhy and what is now Sheridan Road... **History of Rogers Park, Document #25, John D. Cleveland**

I came to Rogers Park in 1880 when I was eight years old. My father had a small farm at 7230 Rogers Avenue and we did small truck farming. As late as 1894 there were large celery patches just west of the Northwestern tracks. Old man Kelly had a cabbage patch over on the Ridge and Old man Stone had a chicken ranch on the Ridge between Greenleaf and Lunt. East of Broadway was all swamp and only a very few people lived there. When I was about twelve after a storm on the lake I would get (sic) early in the dawn and go to the beach to gather driftwood. From this practice we collected enough wood to build a barn... **History of Rogers Park, Document #31, Charles Schubert**

The train station had been built in 1873 and was the neighborhood stop for the Milwaukee Line of the Chicago and Northwestern Railroad. Prior to the construction of the Rogers Park station, one had been built in 1859 opposite the west entrance of Calvary Cemetery on the northern boundary of John O'Leary's farm. East of Ashland Avenue, a second railroad line would later be constructed, but it took until 1885 before the Chicago, Milwaukee and St. Paul completed its ground level tracks from Wilson Avenue in Chicago to Evanston. That line did not have an initial effect on Rogers Park until 1919

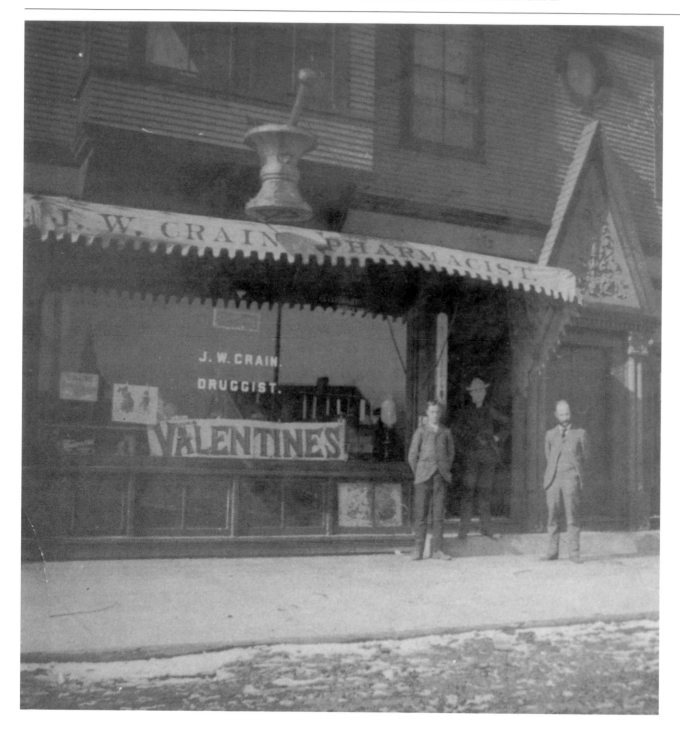

Left: Crain's Drug Store, a Clark Street business, prior to a Valentine's Day in the 1890s.

Opposite top: The Birchwood Depot was one of the stops on the Evanston division of the Chicago, Milwaukee & St. Paul Railway. Built in 1886, it was located on Bryan (now Jarvis) just east of Ashland, near the site of the present Jarvis elevated station.

Opposite left: Civil War veteran John W. Pollard, shown in his uniform of the Grand Army of the Republic (G.A.R.), owned and operated a barbershop at 4316 E. Ravenswood Park (later 7017 N. Ravenswood). He was the first barber in Rogers Park, working from 1886 until 1910.

Opposite right: An Italianate-Second Empire style house, built by Andrew B. Jackson in 1873, is located at 7053 N. Ridge. Jackson was one of the early members of the Rogers Park Land Company. Photograph by Martin J. Schmidt.

when the tracks were elevated, but it did lead to the development of the eastern portion of Rogers Park, including the Birchwood and Germania districts. The Northwestern Elevated Line, which would use the Chicago, Milwaukee and St. Paul tracks, constructed a station at Howard Street in 1908.

The Chicago and Evanston line was built primarily as a suburban railroad. Real estate companies built the elaborate stations and the company did not have to pay a cent for their construction. That is the reason the Wilson Avenue station was so elaborate with parking to Leland Avenue. The Chicago, Milwaukee and St. Paul Railroad was completed to Evanston in 1885, to be used as a freight and commuters railroad. It ran through a district south of Wilson Avenue that was a commercial district and they did a large freight business. **History of Rogers Park, Document #37, Mr. Weiss**

In the late 1870s almost ninety percent of the male residents of Rogers Park worked in Chicago and commuted each day. There was a belief that if the village could become incorporated, it would lead to more services for the residents. However, the farmers who lived west of the Ridge opposed incorporation, and it was through their efforts that West Ridge kept a separate identity from Rogers Park. With Rogers Park's incorporation in 1878, new services were brought to the village, including policemen, a volunteer fire company, and a water plant built by the Rogers Park Water Company. Liquor

was prohibited under Evanston's four-mile rule of 1855.

West Ridge, with its small population prior to the 1870s, had only St. Henry Church located on the north side of Devon west of the Ridge. In 1871, the original building was replaced with a larger one at a cost of $10,000. Additions were made in 1891 and then the current church on the southwest corner was built in 1905. Across the street from the original structure, the Board of Administration of St. Boniface Cemetery built Angel Guardian Orphanage in 1865. The church was also the location of the first school in the area. In addition, the Idelharts, a family in the parish, hired an English tutor for their children. Subsequently, other families sent their children to the Idelhart home to receive an education by the tutor.

St. Henry's school at the Angel Guardian Orphanage was the only school nearby and all the children went there. Children came from miles around and some the children from Niles Center attended school there. **History of Rogers Park, Document #20, Mrs. Kate Lullung** *(sic)*

In 1872, the first school building, the West Side Schoolhouse, was constructed at Indian Boundary Road (Rogers Avenue) and North Robey Street (Damen Avenue). The first directors of the school were J. L. Estes, Peter Muno and Edward Murphy, and the first teacher was Miss Finn. Another school building, the Grand Avenue, or East Side Schoolhouse, was completed in 1878 at

Greenleaf Avenue and Grand Avenue (Ashland Avenue).

With the influx of new residents, there was a growing need for new houses of worship. In 1874, a Methodist church was constructed at Greenleaf and Wolcott. With a major contribution from Patrick Touhy in 1875, St. Catherine Church was built at Touhy and Hilldale (later Wolcott) Avenues.

At that time there wasn't a church and it was partly through my efforts that the first Methodist Church was organized. Mr. Richards who lived in Chicago and was in the region for his health consented to come out to Rogers Park and preach. The first meetings were held in the schoolhouse but their first Christmas was held in the station of the Northwestern Railway and thereafter our meetings were held there until the church was completed on the corner of Greenleaf and Hilldale in 1871 (sic). **History of Rogers Park, Document #23, Mrs. William Kyle**

In the latter part of the nineteenth century, West Ridge was mostly farmland and vegetable gardens. Farmers raised beans, peas, melons and corn to be sold in Chicago. The Luxembourgers constructed greenhouses and three of the area's early pioneers, John Muno, Adam Zender and Peter Reinberg, cultivated vegetables before switching to flowers, a more profitable market, since they could be sold to mourners at Calvary Cemetery. These truck farmers would send their wagons down to Winnemac and Lincoln Avenues to pick up

Top: The East Side Schoolhouse, built in the 1870s, was located on Ashland between Lunt and Greenleaf. With a few additions, it still exists today as Eugene Field Elementary School.

Bottom: The West Side Schoolhouse, also built in the 1870s, was located on Rogers and Damen.

Opposite: Located at Touhy and the lakefront, the Rogers Park Water Company was owned by Hervey Keeler. The utility operated from the 1880s until it was sold in the 1900s.

Top: Rogers Park School, class of 1892.

Right: Rogers Park School, 4th grade October 1894.

Opposite: The Rogers Park tollgate and gatekeeper's house were built in 1869 by Charlie Airs for use by travelers going to and from Calvary Cemetery.

Polish women who would work in the greenhouses for $1.25 a day.

The 1880s and 1890s: Years Prior to Annexation

In the 1880s, the land north of Touhy was covered with burr, white and scrub oak. To the east of Clark, the land was swampy and ditches were needed on both sides of the roads for drainage. There was also the Big Ditch located west of the Chicago, Milwaukee and St. Paul Railroad tracks that ran south from Evanston to Pratt Avenue and east on Pratt to Lake Michigan.

In 1885, North Clark Street was blocked by three tollgates. The most northerly of these was at the Indian Boundary Line where tribute was levied on the long processions that daily passed to Calvary Cemetery. Another was at Rosehill and a third at Graceland where the progress of mourners going to the burial ground was arrested. Indian Boundary Line was a favorite for those who wanted to dodge the tollgate. East of Clark Street there was no street to the north, west of it there was one, Ridge Road, half a mile away. The tollgates were abolished in the late eighties as a result of popular clamor against their maintenance. **History of Rogers Park, Document #22, S. Rogers Touhy**

Homes in Rogers Park had four- to five-foot fences around them to keep out stray cows and horses. The sidewalks were first made of wood, then one-foot square stones, and by the 1890s were made of cement. There were few

paved streets and Sheridan Road was only a sandy stretch of road north of Devon. Until 1890, Western Avenue was a sand track and west of California was prairie. Generally, the streets were paths cut through the woods with tree stumps left standing.

I came to Rogers Park with my father in 1872. Mr. Jackson, of the Rogers Park Land Company, had known my father in the north and when he saw him in Wilmette he told him that he was starting a subdivision in Rogers Park and that he was anxious to get builders into the community. Since father was a carpenter he bought a lot and built a home. It seems that Mr. Jackson had told many other people the same thing and they moved to Rogers Park in the hopes of work. **History of Rogers Park, Document #26, George Carpenter**

Rogers Park experienced a land boom in the 1880s. Real estate developers were attracted to the area and several savings and loan associations were formed. One of the most important new land developers was Franklin H. Doland, who, in 1885, purchased eighteen acres in the town and built his own house on the property. After buying an additional twenty-three acres in 1887, he developed a subdivision from the lake to the Chicago, Milwaukee and St. Paul tracks and from Touhy north to Rogers. His property contained over four miles of sidewalks and four thousand planted trees. Doland also laid down the first six-foot stone sidewalks in Rogers Park, and in 1890 he subdivided his property into lots for the

purchase of houses. Other developers included D. W. and J. M. Kean, J. F. Keaney, and John M. Carlson.

When I came to Rogers Park there were about eight hundred people in the Park, which means within the boundaries of Ridge, Devon, Rogers Avenue and the Lake. I built the first house in Birchwood and that was my own residence on the corner of Sheridan and Touhy. The district was not very swampy at that time but there were springs everywhere. Touhy had only wooden sidewalks and they were not continuous. I built the waterworks in 1889 and built almost six miles of mains although my contract only called for a minimum of five miles…The sewerage system was installed at the same time that the water works were laid. **History of Rogers Park, Document #41, H. E. Keeler**

In 1887 I lived at Pratt and the Lake…Sheridan Road was just a sandy stretch then. South of Devon it was a regular road but north of Devon it was just trees, willow bushes and grass…When I first came to Rogers Park the people went to Evanston and downtown to get their groceries. Lampke's grocery and meat market was the first store… **History of Rogers Park, Document #30, Peter Karels**

As noted earlier, after incorporation, a waterworks, a village hall, a fire department and schoolhouses were established. The waterworks opened in 1889, and by 1890 there were six miles of water pipes being laid in the vil-

lage. The first mains were built on Sheridan and Clark, and between the two streets there were water mains on Touhy, Greenleaf, Lunt, Morse, Farwell and Pratt, as well as one on Ridge and some of the streets between Clark and Ridge. A new school was built at Lunt and Grand Avenue (Ashland Avenue). At first, only two rooms of the school were built, but as the years passed, there were expansions of the original structure and, by 1899, Eugene Field School was completed. Armstrong School, built in 1912 west of Ridge on Estes Avenue, became the first public school located in West Ridge.

In the early 1890s, there was growing activity that led to improvement of public works and utilities, as well as transportation. In July 1891, the Edison Electric Company agreed to build and operate the Chicago and Evanston Electric Railway Company. At that same time, there were plans to build the Chicago, Evanston and Southern Elevated Railway that would connect Chicago, from Jackson Park and Englewood on the far south side, to Rogers Park and then Evanston. The elevated line had a fare of $.05 and operated on tracks suspended twelve feet above ground.

The Incorporation of West Ridge and the Growth of Birchwood

As Rogers Park continued to grow, the decision was made in 1890 by residents of West Ridge to incorporate as a village. One of the main reasons for incorporation was that West Ridge residents could not get elected to the Rogers Park Village Board. In addition, Rogers Park had passed an ordinance that expanded the scope of Evanston's four-mile rule to include the saloons in West Ridge. The new vil-

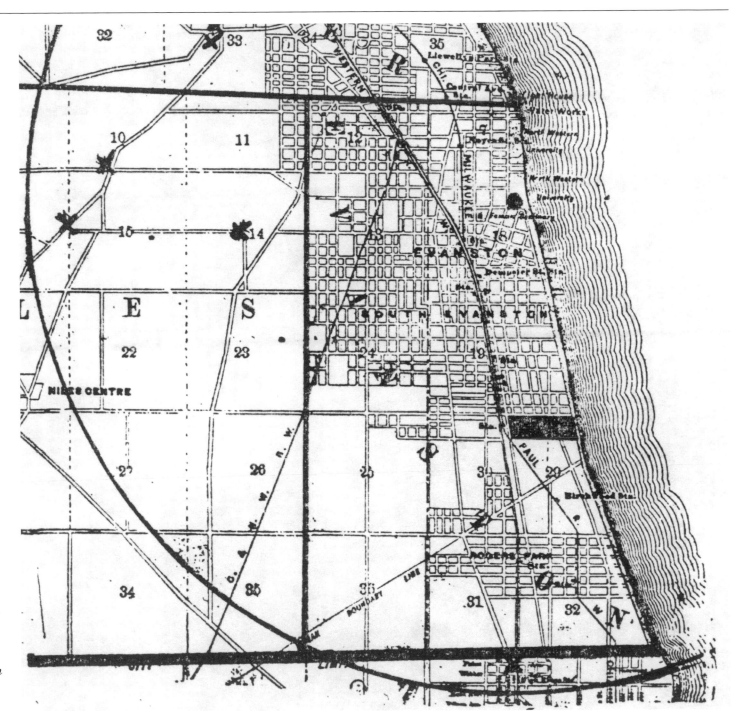

This 1891 map shows the proposed boundary for saloon restriction within a four-mile radius of Northwestern University.

lage of West Ridge declared that its new boundaries would extend along the Ridge from Devon to Touhy and west to Kedzie. The West Ridge Village Board also began to improve the roads by paving Lunt from Ridge to Western, and decided to receive water from the Rogers Park waterworks through water mains on Ridge north of Columbia. Farms and greenhouses were the primary businesses of the village. Early residents described the land as good for growing between the Ridge and California Avenue, but swampy and sandy to the west, with fresh water springs and deposits of clay.

During the period when West Ridge was developing, changes were also taking place in the northeastern portion of Rogers Park known as the Birchwood district. The area along Lake Michigan, north of Touhy, had its own local government. It was a sandbank filled with birch and oak trees and no paved streets. Birchwood was primarily made up of farms, with a few houses. Since it had not been drained, rising and falling Lake Michigan waters caused the district to be swampy during much of the year. Still, it was an attractive, wooded district. Sheridan Road was named for Civil War General Philip Sheridan, a friend of Patrick Touhy, and when it was laid out and people began seeing it as a route along the Lake between Chicago and the towns further north, a movement began to develop the Birchwood area.

In 1888, William Hatterman moved to the Birchwood area from the Near North Side of Chicago and built his house just west of the Chicago, Milwaukee and St. Paul tracks between Rogers Avenue and Howard. Farms surrounded his property. John Ure's dairy farm extended east of the Ridge from Rogers to

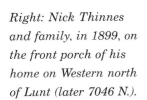 *Right: Nick Thinnes and family, in 1899, on the front porch of his home on Western north of Lunt (later 7046 N.).*

Opposite top: By 1900 many members of the Luxembourg Brotherhood were successful greenhouse owners. These included the Winandy brothers who were also greenhouse builders, locally and throughout the country.

Opposite bottom: Nick Thinnes and worker in his greenhouse in the 7000 block of N. Western around 1900.

A. W. Wilson.   R. F. Thorogood.   C. W. Jennings.   H. D. Greene.   H. E. Rounds.   J. L. Nelson.

E. Dewey.   E. Ament.   C. W. Roberts.   W. Brandt.   D. W. McNulty.   J. Snyder.

H. R. Sampson.   Rev. F. V. Cleveland   T. F. Burns.   E. D. Cove.   A. F. Karadon.   C. W. Beperty.

Opposite: Civil War veterans in Rogers Park formed the Cumberland Post, a branch of the Grand Army of the Republic, in the 1890s. They met in Phoenix Hall on the northwest corner of Lunt and Clark.

Right: Cornelius H. Ceperly in his Civil War uniform. After the war, he was a commander of Post 737. He was also a prominent builder in Rogers Park.

Bottom: Grand Army of the Republic Cumberland Post No. 737 booklet cover dated 1909.

Cumberland Post No. 737
Department of Illinois
G. A. R.
ROGERS PARK, CHICAGO

Meets in Phoenix Hall, northwest corner N. Clark St.
and Greenleaf Ave., the second and fourth Friday
evenings of each month except June, July, August and September, when meetings will be
held only on the second Friday evenings.

Howard and east of Clark Street. There was an area north of Howard known as "No Man's Land," or Germania, and this section would, by 1915, become part of Chicago. There were so few residents in the Birchwood area in the 1880s that there was no water or sewerage service, so two windmills were constructed to supply water. A friend of Hatterman from Philadelphia sent a dynamo that was attached to one of the windmills, providing electricity to Birchwood residents five years before wires were extended into Rogers Park.

The rambling Hatterman house was at the south end of the tract. Beside it was the big horse barn. Over there, the windmill. And in the midst of the foliage a pond was fed from a spring, as well as an apple orchard and grape vines. **North Shore News, January 23, 1931**

The Hattermans called their land "Willow Lea," and when they moved there, they added to the natural foliage with a wide variety of bushes and vines. They brought in golden pheasants, foxes, owls and eagles and imported flowers and bulbs from Holland. William Hatterman filled his yard with fruit trees. Children from Rogers Park would come to play and eat the fruit. During the winter he had toboggans and other toys for the children and they could skate on his pond. Later, as president of the Rogers Park Board, Hatterman started the Farwell bathing beach and installed the first lifesaving station. He also began the school gardens at Eugene Field School on Lunt and on Ashland.

That portion of Rogers Park which seems likely to grow most rapidly is that centering around the Birchwood Beach station. The improved train service just adopted on the Chicago, Milwaukee and St. Paul road will have a favorable influence here as well as at other points. Several new dwellings are being erected or are under contract, the sewer and water systems are to be extended and a new railway station is talked of. **The Evanston Index, May 6, 1892**

The Annexation Movement

The population of Rogers Park began to grow rapidly, and by 1893 there were 3,500 residents in the village as well as a thriving business district. Although a major fire destroyed many of the businesses along Clark Street near the train station on Ravenswood in 1894, the area was quickly rebuilt with brick buildings.

Then, in the early 1890s, there was continuing discussion about whether Rogers Park and West Ridge should seek or accept annexation to the city of Chicago. The upcoming Columbian Exposition, Chicago's World's Fair of 1893, was one of the main reasons for the growing support in favor of annexation. Many residents of the two villages thought that the Exposition would bring prosperity to those living within the borders of Chicago. Others opposed annexation because of expected higher city taxes for schools and other services.

The Rogers Park Annexation Club was formed in January 1893. In March, a petition with 239 names was submitted to the Cook County Court asking that the citizens of Chicago, and Rogers Park, vote on the issue of annexation at the April 4, 1893 election. In the weeks before the vote, there were heated discussions at meetings in Rogers Park around the issues of new property and school taxes, improved water supply, and additional and improved police and fire protection. On March 10, 1893, the Village Board discussed annexation at its meeting.

The die is cast; the fight is on. Last Tuesday a petition signed by 239 names was presented to the county court asking that the people of Chicago and Rogers Park vote on the question of annexation at the election to be held April 4. From now on, the subject will be canvassed and argued between those who favor and those who oppose the movement…it is a very important question, and the greatest care should be taken in considering it. It seems to us, after hearing arguments on both sides and noting the present flourishing conditions of the other suburbs which have been gathered under Chicago's wing, that, all things considered, it may be a step in the right direction…In a general way, it seems to us that it will be a means of saving a great deal of money to taxpayers in the long run and enable us to have certain improvements, such as street lighting, more ample police and fire protection, et cetera, speedily carried out, which does not look likely under village government. **History of Rogers Park, Document #3, Open Letter for Annexation, March 10, 1893**

On April 4, 1893, by a majority of 112 votes, Rogers Park voted in favor of annexation. In West Ridge, the vote was much closer due to strong concerns about continuing ability to legally operate the taverns in the village once it became a part of Chicago. Despite those continuing concerns, the farmers of West Ridge, by a majority of only ten votes, approved annexation to the city. In 1893, both Rogers Park and West Ridge became the northernmost neighborhoods of the city of Chicago.

Annexation went through all right up here. There were some that didn't want it. They said that it would bring in saloons. And of course the taxes were higher the very next year. The higher taxes may have hurt some, but there are always those kind of people and I don't recall many. Of course there were a few. The improvements began coming in right away. **History of West Rogers Park, Document #1, Dominick Schreiber**

Julius Soerns, one of the first mail carriers in Rogers Park, c. 1890.

Sheridan Rd.

Eugene Field School

Birchwood Country Club.

Seasons Greeting from Rogers Park Chicago. Ill.

"The Hillside"

Lake Michigan On a Windy Morning

The Beach

Congregational Church

655.

New North Side Neighborhoods
1894 - 1919

Annexation to Chicago meant that Rogers Park and West Ridge residents would receive new city services for their taxes, including water, gas, sewerage, electricity, telephones, police and fire protection, and schools. Telephone service began on March 11, 1896, and Chicago installed streetlight posts, sewers, cement sidewalks, and new fire hydrants, as well as a four-room addition at Eugene Field School.

*With the annexation of Rogers Park to Chicago many improvements were put through. Gas was installed. It was not then supposed that Rogers Park would ever be furnished with electrical current, but it came in about 1895, as well as the telephone system. The first installment was thirty phones. F. H. Doland's Sub-division was made in 1889, Birchwood Subdivision in 1890, and the subdivisions all sold out very rapidly by lots and also by blocks, the blocks being purchased by speculators who afterwards sold them out lot by lot. **History of Rogers Park, Document #42, Lloyd G. Kirkland***

*When Chicago decided to take Rogers Park under her protective wing (in 1893) she made a wise move. By annexation, Rogers Park's two schools, which are ranked among the best in the country, became city property. And, these are perhaps the greatest acquisitions gained by the transfer of title of the village on the north shore to the city government. **Chicago Evening Post**, February 23, 1894*

However, there was an indication in 1894 that Rogers Park and West Ridge were still considered as "outsiders" by some Chicago business enterprises. Shortly after annexation, residents of Rogers Park were forced to stage a rebellion against the North Chicago Street Railway Company in what came to be known as the "Home-Made Transfer War." The "war"

Opposite: A holiday postcard from the early 1900s of selected Rogers Park scenes.

Top left: Riders in a special horse-drawn streetcar in 1912. The first horsecar line reached Devon via Clark in 1889 after the annexation of Lake View. Horsecars and cable cars were completely replaced by electric streetcars in Chicago in 1906. Chicago Historical Society: ICHI-05464

Top right: A muddy winter streetcar stop in 1911 looking south on Clark from Howard.
Chicago Historical Society: ICHI-29403 Daily News - DN-008914

Left: An open-air trolley, in the early 1900s, operated by Chicago Union Traction from the car barn at Clark and Schubert. It ran along Evanston Avenue (now Broadway) through Lakeview, Edgewater and Rogers Park to Central Street in Evanston.

was ignited when riders on Clark Street in Rogers Park were forced to pay an extra fare to travel into the city.

After the World Columbian Exposition in 1893, the Street Railway Company had extended its Clark Street service to Rogers Park. At first, the residents of Rogers Park were pleased with the new means of transportation. However, that joy changed to anger when they learned that transportation czar, Charles T. Yerkes, was going to require that Rogers Park riders pay an additional fare. Those riders, who usually boarded the horse-drawn railway at Estes Avenue and Clark, as well as those from the communities of Edgewater and Argyle Park, were asked to pay an extra fare once the street railway crossed Graceland Avenue (Irving Park Road). Since they were a part of the city's population, these riders resented the new requirement to pay this additional fee.

Led by Harlow W. Phelps, the son-in-law of early settler Robert Kyle, the citizens of Rogers Park rebelled against this new charge. Phelps and his supporters organized the Universal Transfer Alliance. The Alliance took the matter to court, but even after the judge ruled in their favor, the Railway Company ignored the decision. Thus, the group decided to take matters into their own hands. Armed with a batch of homemade transfers, they boarded the cars at the transfer point and forced the reluctant conductors to accept those transfers. They were victorious in their struggle with the North Chicago Street Railway Company.

Due to a national economic depression in the mid 1890s, Rogers Park grew slowly after annexation. Yet the neighborhood infrastructure continued to be developed, including paved streets, new lighting and other utilities

Above: Postal employees stand in front of the Rogers Park Post Office on the northeast corner of Greenleaf and Clark around 1900.

Bottom: The combined headquarters of the Rogers Park Police (originally the 45th Precinct) and Fire Departments was located on the southeast corner of Estes and Clark in 1900.

Opposite top left: The northeast corner of Devon and Clark in 1910. Chicago Historical Society: ICHI-25987 Charles R. Childs postcard

Opposite top right: Clark Street north of Lunt in the early 1900s.

Opposite bottom left: Peter Tres, a shoemaker and repairer of boots, is shown with his sons in 1896. His shop was located at 4843 Clark (later 7048 N.)

Opposite bottom right: The Peter Weimeschkirch undertaking business at 4861 Clark (later 7066 N.) was established in 1888. It operated as a family business for almost 100 years. Their ambulance also functioned as a hearse.

Right: Weimeschkirch Undertaking ad c. 1900.

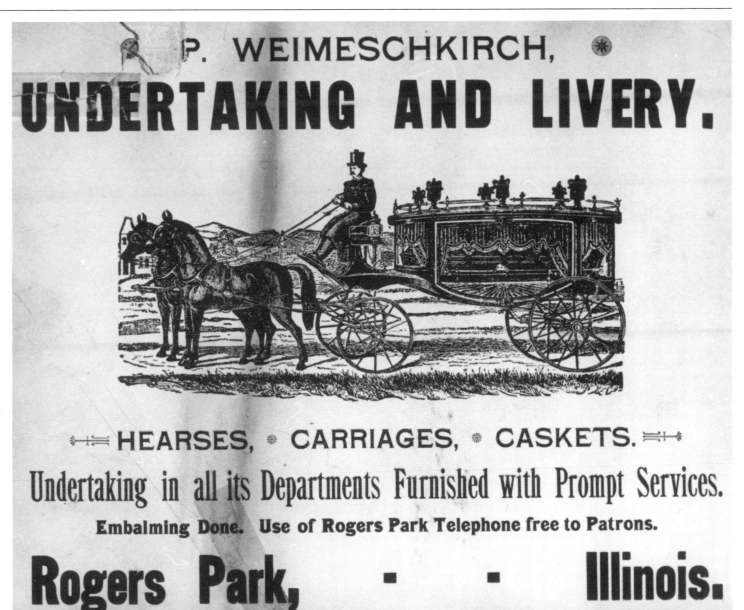

P. WEIMESCHKIRCH,

UNDERTAKING AND LIVERY.

HEARSES, CARRIAGES, CASKETS.

Undertaking in all its Departments Furnished with Prompt Services.

Embalming Done. Use of Rogers Park Telephone free to Patrons.

Rogers Park, - - Illinois.

that were developed for the steady increase of new residents who purchased houses throughout the neighborhood. In 1893, the first police station was established in Rogers Park in the village hall on Estes and Clark, along with the fire station.

The firefighters became very important to the new neighborhood when, on the morning of August 8, 1894, a major disaster occurred around the Clark Street business area. According to an article in the July 4, 1976 <u>Lerner News</u>: "Water for fire fighting in those days was purchased from a private company, which usually pumped the water up into a water tower for the night supply. That morning it was 85 degrees in the shade, and residents trying to keep cool had already used the standpipe water supply when the fire engines arrived. The disastrous conflagration started in a lumber planing mill at Greenleaf and East Ravenswood Avenue. Although the fire engines arrived quickly, the mains were dry and a whole block of the area was destroyed." However, within a short time the area was rebuilt with brick buildings.

The amount of building in past year has been remarkable. Most of the houses of this year have been of a superior type, costing from $3,000 to $10,000. The Birchwood district has several very elegant houses. King's and Carlson's subdivisions in the south and south east have also had a boom in a fine class of houses. The west side has not been neglected either. Mr. Overdier is building in the southwest part. **Rogers Park News Herald, November 2, 1894**

Above: This building, at 702 Greenleaf (later 1774 W.), on the northeast corner at Ravenswood, was the first location of the Phillip Bank.

Right: This 1916 program booklet from St. Paul's Episcopal Church included numerous advertisements of Rogers Park and Chicago businesses.

The Schubert Brothers Grocery Store at 704 Greenleaf (later 1772 W.) in 1910.

The most important issue of the period was the conflict that developed between the residents of West Ridge and Rogers Park over the creation of park districts in the newly annexed neighborhoods. It became known as the "Cabbage Head War" of 1896. The controversy may have begun in 1895 when a law concerning parks, passed by the Illinois legislature, would become the basis for the creation of park districts by Rogers Park and West Ridge. The proponents of the new North Shore Park District saw it as providing new opportunities for land development, the paving of Sheridan Road and Ridge Avenues, and the development of beachfront properties.

At the same time, a group of West Ridge residents that included H. D. Capitain and John D. Cleveland began a legal movement to create the Ridge Avenue Park District that would serve to improve West Ridge and Rogers Park, west of the railroad tracks to Ridge Boulevard.

Residents of West Ridge opposed the North Shore Park District because they resented the attempt of east siders, or "silk stockings" to use their tax monies to build parks and develop land in the eastern section of Rogers Park, especially along Lake Michigan. The conflict pitted such individuals as attorney Lloyd Kirkland and his supporters of the new park district against the West Ridge residents. Kirkland wanted to have an election on the issue. State Senator Jimmy Barbour, another supporter of the District and resident of Rogers Park, was reported to have compared the West Ridgers to the cabbages, or "cabbage heads" grown by the West Ridge farmers. This comment was also considered demeaning to the German farmers of the Ridge. In response to

Kirkland's move for an election and to Barbour's comments, the farmers began a parade, with cabbage heads attached to poles, to Kirkland's home on Sheridan.

On April 14, 1896, voters in West Ridge and the western part of Rogers Park gave almost unanimous support for the Ridge Avenue Park District. Meanwhile, a majority of voters in the eastern part of Rogers Park voted not to create the North Shore Park District because they feared a significant increase in taxes to pay for parks along the lake and the creation of Sheridan Road as a boulevard. The opponents of the North Shore Park District felt that it would only benefit those who owned large tracts of real estate near the lake. As a result of the vote, Ridge Avenue was paved, funds were used to purchase Indian Boundary Park, and other streets in West Ridge were improved.

I doubt if the Ridge Avenue Park District would ever have been formed if the spirit of West Ridge had not been aroused. The thing came directly from a remark by a speaker at a meeting held in Rogers Park which West Ridge people attended. The matter discussed there was the formation of the North Shore Park District. Senator Barbour, who was just Jimmy Barbour then, got up to make a speech and alluded to the people of West Ridge as "cabbage heads." That got the farmers mad and they organized their own park district. **History of West Rogers Park, Document #4a, Judge Joseph Fitch**

While the "Home Made Transfer War," and the "Cabbage Head War" were the issues that

attracted the most attention in the 1890s, other important events also occurred in the early years after annexation. On February 22, 1895, Peter Phillip, son of one of Rogers Park's earliest residents and an active citizen of Rogers Park, opened the neighborhood's first bank. The Phillip State Bank and Trust Company was first located at Schubert's corner at 1774 W. Greenleaf Avenue (at Ravenswood), and then moved to 7005 N. Clark. According to the <u>Chicago Tribune</u>: "It was a half million dollar memorial to the one who met the banking needs of his neighbors as the traffic of Chicago replaced the truck farms" (March 16, 1930, p. 1).

Consequently, in 1895, I started a private bank, which was the outgrowth of my feed and grain business and the Building and Loan Association. It is true that we did have the first safe and vault in Rogers Park…By 1915, the bank had expanded so much that we were able to recapitalize as a state bank. **History of Rogers Park, Document #21, Peter Phillip**

Also in 1895, the Milwaukee Line of the Chicago and Northwestern Railroad opened a new railroad station at Lunt and Ravenswood. While the railroad had been providing service to Rogers Park for thirty years, the new station was a sign that annexation would bring more modern facilities to the neighborhood.

Thus, Rogers Park and West Ridge had grown from small villages, with undeveloped sections of prairie and farmland in the mid-1800s to incorporated villages, and, finally, annexed sections of the far north side of Chicago

Top left: An ornate illustration depicting Sheridan Road and Lake Michigan's North Shore. Chicago Historical Society: ICHI 17821

Top right: Sheridan Road looking south from Morse in 1905.

Bottom: The southwest corner of Farwell and Sheridan in 1917 prior to the neighborhood's construction boom.

by 1900. The population and construction growth of the new neighborhoods became quite significant over the next thirty years.

Rogers Park at the Turn of the Century

At the beginning of the 1900s, Rogers Park and West Ridge remained sparsely populated extensions of Chicago. The concentration of housing and businesses in Rogers Park was around the train station at Greenleaf and Ravenswood Avenues, while farmers and their greenhouses were located along and west of Ridge to Western.

To the west of Western there was only prairie and farmland, as well as some brickyards along the western limits near Touhy Avenue. The brickyards constructed in West Ridge were able to use the natural deposits of sand and clay in the region. After the turn of the century, around 1905, the National Brick Company bought land south of Touhy, between Kedzie Avenue and California. The construction of the Sanitary District Canal in 1909 provided the clay that the brickyard needed for its business. The brickyards brought new workers, primarily Germans and Scandinavians into the area and they built small cottages near their workplaces.

There was renewed interest in the approval of a park district for Rogers Park. A new referendum on the creation of the North Shore Park District was passed, by a vote of 249 to 203, on May 10, 1900. This referendum aided in the development of the land east of Clark, from Devon to the northern city limits in the Birchwood district. One of the major opponents of the creation of the North Shore Park District

was S. Rogers Touhy, the grandson of Philip Rogers. He was concerned about the designation of Sheridan as a boulevard because that would shift funeral processions to Calvary Cemetery from Sheridan to Clark and would increase the traffic on that street. In fact, the Rogers Park Village Board, as early as 1891, had expressed its objection to the large number of funeral processions on Sheridan.

Although the Northwestern Elevated Line had been extended to Wilson Avenue in 1900 on the old Chicago, Milwaukee and St. Paul tracks, it would take several more years before that line would reach Rogers Park, and then Evanston.

Above: Workers in front of the National Brickyard on Kedzie north of Touhy in 1910.

Opposite top left: An "elevated" train stands at the Rogers Park station in c.1900 at Morse Avenue, the present site of the Rogers Park/Morse elevated station.

Opposite top right: Looking south as an "elevated" train approaches the Birchwood stop in 1913, present site of the Jarvis elevated station. Chicago Historical Society: Daily News - DN-61524

Opposite bottom left: Chicago, Milwaukee & St. Paul train with steam locomotive sits on a freight track near Howard.

Opposite bottom right: Chicago & Northwestern Depot at ground level at Greenleaf and Ravenswood in 1905. The tracks and station were later elevated.

Elevating the tracks south of present day Loyola station about 1915. Property of Loyola University is on the right. The original St. Ignatius Church is in the upper left. The Granada Theatre was built on this site in 1926.

The Northwestern Elevated...was opened for traffic as far north as Wilson Avenue on May 31, 1900. It was operated around the loop from its inception. The Ravenswood branch was opened in 1907 and the following year the main line was extended to Evanston, operating over tracks of the C.M.&St.P. Railroad. The line was extended to Wilmette in 1912. At the time the Northwestern Elevated opened for traffic what is known as the Wilson Avenue district, one of the most populous residence and business sections of the city, was largely a cow pasture. A photograph taken of the corner of Wilson and Broadway about the time the "L" opened shows a frame cottage with a pump to furnish the water supply and a cow grazing in the yard. **History of Rogers Park, Document #39, *From Intramural to L.1923***

On July 1, 1907, Chicago authorized the electrification of the Chicago, Milwaukee and St. Paul tracks from Graceland (Irving Park) to Howard, but did not require that the tracks be elevated. As part of the agreement with the city, the "L" (with tracks at ground level from Wilson to Howard until 1922) was required to provide twenty-four-hour service from all stops, including Loyola, Morse, Birchwood, and Howard. In 1908, the Howard Street station was opened.

The extension of the Howard Branch of the L system to Howard Street in 1908 was especially welcomed by the residents of the eastern part of the community. Although

Birchwood, located in northeastern Rogers Park, and the remainder of the eastern part of the community had profited to some extent by earlier booms, there were still vacant lots in Birchwood offered for sale to the public. Howard and Loyola were two undeveloped areas which now grew rapidly. **The Elevated System and the Growth of Northern Chicago, *p. 34***

New Community Institutions in Rogers Park and West Ridge

In 1902, the Rogers Park Lutheran Church was organized at the Phoenix Hall at the northwest corner of Greenleaf and Clark. Two years later, when the Congregational Church wanted to expand to new facilities, the Lutheran Church purchased that property. Then the Rogers Park Lutheran Church moved to new facilities on Morse Avenue in 1912. In 1905, St. Jerome's first Church was built on the northwest corner of Morse and Paulina.

Between 1905 and 1906 St. Jerome enlarged its physical plant as it offered its parishioners more services and accommodated an expanding population. The centerpiece of the parish complex is the church located on the southwest corner of Lunt and Paulina Street with its imposing Romanesque edifice. Built in 1916 under the direction of architect Charles H. Prindiville, the structure was enlarged in 1934. In addition to the church, the parish complex included a school, convent, and rectory. **Reading Your Neighborhood: A History of East Rogers Park**

The Jesuits and Benedictine Sisters in Chicago decided to build religious and educational institutions in the recently annexed portion of Chicago. One of those institutions was St. Scholastica Academy, which opened its doors on Ridge Boulevard in 1906.

Saint Scholastica Academy is a continuation of the old Saints Benedict and Scholastica Academy on Hill and Orleans Street, a "young ladies finishing school" built soon after the Chicago Fire... Following northward migration of their patrons, the Sisters chose Rogers Park as the site for their new Motherhouse, which, according to Benedictine traditions, was on the only eminence available in the "City of the Plaines" -- namely, the Ridge, or old shore line of Lake Michigan. The new institution grew rapidly, keeping pace with the development of Chicago, until in 1925 a building was erected exclusively for the purposes of a school, while the old structure was devoted to the use of the convent and novitiate. **History of Rogers Park, Document #19, The Diamond Jubilee, 1920**

In 1906, the Chicago Jesuits also saw the opportunity to buy land in Rogers Park to build new schools and churches. They purchased nineteen and one-half acres of land from the Chicago, Milwaukee and St. Paul Railroad at the northeast corner of Sheridan and Devon Avenue at a cost of $161,255. The land, formerly known as Cape Hayes and named for a nineteenth century lake captain, would become the home of the St.

Opposite top left: The original St. Paul By-the-Lake Episcopal Church was built in 1886 on Lunt east of Clark. It was torn down in the 1920s and rebuilt on the northwest corner of Estes and Ashland.

Opposite top right: The original St. Ignatius Church, 1907-1917, was located at on Sheridan north of Devon. The Granada Theatre was built on this site in 1926.

Opposite lower left: The original St. Jerome Church, built in 1905, was located on the northwest corner of Morse and Paulina. The new church building, one block north at Lunt and Paulina, continues to serve the neighborhood.

Opposite lower right: The Rogers Park Congregational Church, built in 1905, is located on the southeast corner of Morse and Ashland. This picture is from a post card with a Chicago postmark of 1914.

Top left: The original Rogers Park Presbyterian Church, built 1910-12, is located just north of the present church at 7059 N. Greenview.

Top right: Loyola Academy, a boys' high school, was built in 1906 and was one of the original buildings on the Loyola University campus.

Lower right: Convent and Academy of St. Scholastica, 7416-30 N. Ridge, in 1925. This institution still operates today as a girl's high school and the motherhouse of the Benedictine Order.

Ignatius Parish. The church opened its doors for worshippers in February 1907, with the new building providing seating for four hundred parishioners in its white and green wood frame structure. In 1909, the Jesuits built a grammar school at 6558 Sheridan, and in 1911 the church bought land at 1300 W. Loyola where it constructed a new school building for the St. Ignatius elementary school that opened in 1912. As the parish grew to more than three hundred families who were members of the parish, so did the desire for a new church, and in 1917 the congregation moved to 6559 Glenwood. (The old church at Cape Hayes was dismantled in 1921.) Later, after the parish had moved to its new church, the former land at Cape Hayes would become the location for the Granada Theatre in 1926.

The Jesuit order opened Loyola Academy for Boys in 1908, housed at Dumbach Hall. Also, in 1909, St. Ignatius College became eligible for university status and obtained a charter to change its name to Loyola University. Its new Lake Shore campus on the grounds where Cape Hayes had been located included such buildings as Dumbach Hall (built in 1909), Michael Cudahy Science Hall (built in 1912), and Elizabeth Cudahy Memorial Library (built in 1930).

The opening of the Loyola L station in 1908 made it possible for many second- and third-generation Irish Americans to move to the developing Loyola section of Rogers Park, and this led to residential construction of two-story brick apartment buildings near Loyola University and St. Ignatius Church.

I came to the Loyola district in 1907. The place where the college (Loyola University) stands now used to be used as a picnic ground a long time ago...There used to be a real estate office, but it was only an old shack, at the Elevated and Sheridan Road where Henderson's Real Estate office is now (established in 1912). Sheridan Road was pretty muddy just there and when you stepped off the door sill onto the plank laid down in the front door, you splashed yourself with mud. **History of Rogers Park, Document #53, John C. Dillon**

When I came to Rogers Park for the first time, on a tour of investigation for a site of the new college, there was nothing but sand, scrub oaks, and bush in the Loyola district...This trip was made sometime in 1903. Our committee went up to Wilson Avenue on the L, which was as far as the line went then, and from that point we took a buggy on up to Rogers Park...There was no sentiment connected with the selection of the site for the college. The land was cheap and seemed to be a good buy. This particular piece of land was called Hayes Point...There was a frame house standing on the south side of Hayes Avenue (Loyola Avenue) at the time the land was purchased...The land in the original purchase did not extend to Devon on Sheridan Road, but ended at the south side of the present Granada Theater, leaving that corner lot where the gasoline station is now, vacant. Our land did go to Devon east of the elevated tracks and as far east as it goes now. **History of Rogers Park, Document #49, Father Siedenburg**

One of St. Ignatius' most distinguished parishioners was Edward P. Brennan, who is credited with creating Chicago's modern street numbering system. The problem for the city was that as it annexed new sections throughout the latter part of the nineteenth century, each area retained its own numbering system. Brennan's proposed method of numbering the streets passed the Chicago City Council in 1908 and went into effect in 1909.

Among the most significant accomplishments of Brennan's system was the establishment of State and Madison as the ground zero points of a new numbering system. The basic unit of this new numbering system was 800, which signified one mile...Brennan is also responsible for the system by which odd or even numbered addresses indicate on which side of a street one lives (north and west sides have even numbered addresses while south and east sides are signified by odd numbers). Brennan also vastly simplified street naming by insisting on one name per street and ultimately named hundreds of Chicago's streets himself. **The Historian, Spring, 1998**

In addition to the educational and religious institutions in the neighborhoods, one of the most influential community organizations was the Rogers Park Woman's Club founded in the fall of 1891. It grew from an initial membership of ten women to over nine hundred members by the early 1940s. On June 14, 1916, the cornerstone was laid for the Club's building at 7077 N. Ashland on the northwest corner of Estes and Ashland. By 1894, the Woman's Club had opened a "library and reading room" that would later become a branch library in the Chicago Public Library system, located on Clark between Greenleaf and Lunt. From 1923 until after World War II, the library was located at 1731 W. Greenleaf, then back to its original location of Clark after a fire in the 1950s, and finally to its present location on Clark, between Morse and Farwell.

The Woman's Club also provided a domestic science class to neighborhood residents in 1899, and, from 1915 until 1940, assumed responsibility for the Senn High School lunchroom.

The Edgewater Golf Course and the Wallen Subdivision

West of the land that the Jesuits bought at Cape Hayes, the Edgewater Golf Club had its first site in 1898. The Club was located on a fifty-five-acre tract south of Devon and west of Sheridan and Evanston Avenue (Broadway). In 1899, the Western Golf Association was established and the Edgewater Golf Club was one of its fifteen charter members.

Top: Laying the cornerstone for the Rogers Park Woman's Club, at 7077 N. Ashland, on June 14, 1916. The Club operated from this building for seventy of their 106 years.

Bottom: In 1915 the Rogers Park Library was located at 6957 N. Clark and remained there until 1922. Library service was established by the Rogers Park Woman's Club in 1894. Club members acted as librarians and books were donated by local residents.

About the fall of 1896, five men laid out about three holes on the west side of Evanston Avenue, now Broadway. Here, on two sandy, turfless blocks, including an alleyway with a full complement of ash cans, bounded by Thorndale on the south and Norwood Street on the north, these hardy golf pioneers played. **History of Rogers Park, Document #17a, J. B. Merkels**

But, those who were interested in golf sought a better location, and, in the fall of 1897, the five members secured a one-year lease on thirty acres bounded by Devon and Southport Avenue (later Glenwood) and Sheridan. They erected a small clubhouse in 1898, and by then there were twenty-five members. The original nine-hole golf course had measured 2,804 yards, and was increased to 3,008 yards by 1900.

However, in the early 1900s, real estate men were encroaching on the property of the golf course, and the founding members began to seek a larger location for the Club. In 1910 they settled on a new site bounded by Pratt Avenue, Albion, Ridge and Western. The new clubhouse, and an eighteen-hole golf course, opened in its new location in May 1911.

The opening of the golf course along Ridge Boulevard also created an opportunity for the construction of new homes. William Wallen was the developer of a subdivision south of the Edgewater Golf Course. From 1913 through the 1920s, Wallen constructed almost seventy new apartment buildings.

The section south of the Edgewater Golf Course to Devon Avenue is building up solidly as an apartment house section. They have, of course, a fine view over the green of the golf course, though as it is a private course, they cannot play there… The section, just south of the golf course, has developed within the last sixteen months. Inside lots are selling there for $150 a front foot. A new sixty-apartment building is now under construction there.
___Lincolnite___*, December 17, 1925*

The Development of West Ridge

Between 1895 and 1910, West Ridge had grown from a small community of 127 residential structures to a population of three thousand. This influx of residents increased the need for a public school. Although the East Side and West Side schools were built in Rogers Park in the nineteenth century, there were no public schools in West Ridge. Neighborhood residents were able to get Chicago to build a new elementary school named Armstrong School. Located on Estes just west of Ridge, it opened to students in 1912 and its first principal was Miss Azile Reynolds.

I came to the school in 1912 when it was opened. At that time the school was located in a grove of oak trees with a great deal of brush and woods…The oak trees were our distinguishing feature and the place was called the Oak Grove before the school was built. The people of Rogers Park used it for a picnic grove…The site was chosen because of the high location of the ground

Opposite top: Looking east across the original Edgewater Golf Course toward Sheridan Road. The golf course opened in the late 1890s near the current location of Loyola University. The original St. Ignatius Church is seen in the upper right hand corner shortly after it was built in 1907.

Opposite bottom: The prairie style Edgewater Golf clubhouse, is shown in 1915. Located near Pratt and Ridge, the clubhouse was torn down in the late 1960s and the land is now part of Warren Park.

Top: Armstrong School kindergarten class of 1914.

Bottom: The northeast corner of Devon and Western in 1914.

*just west of Ridge Boulevard...It was
thought better to put the school west of
Ridge since the population in West Ridge
had grown west...The district west of us
during the war was used for war gardens.
Before (World War I), the land had been
sold out in small lots through magazine
subscriptions.* **History of West Rogers
Park, Document #11, Miss Azile
Reynolds**

On August 28, 1912, the Ridge Avenue Park
District, which was created in 1896, decided to
acquire land in the area where Philip Rogers
had first built his house in the 1830s. The Ridge
Avenue Park District Board approved the purchase of the land in 1915. The land was designated as Indian Boundary Park on October 25,
1916, to commemorate the 1816 treaty with the
Native Americans and the creation of the Indian Boundary Line. The park would be located
at 2500 W. Lunt, west of Western and bounded
by Estes and Lunt on the north and south, and
Rockwell and Campbell Avenues on the west
and east. By the early 1930s, the park included
a field house, zoo, tennis courts, a wading pool,
and extensive landscaping. The park also contained a bronze plaque dedicated to Philip
Rogers, a monument dedicated to local veterans of World War I, and a gray granite boulder
with a plaque dedicated to the Potawatomi Indians.

West Ridge also became home to the Chicago Fresh Air Hospital that was built in 1912
on twenty acres of the Peter Gouden farm at
the southwest corner of Howard and Western.
Doctors from Augustana Hospital wanted to
build a sanitarium for tuberculosis patients

Opposite top: Two of the Wiltgen sons work their farm, located near Jarvis and California, with a horse-drawn plow in 1916. Looking east toward Western, The Chicago Fresh Air Hospital, a tuberculosis sanitarium, can be seen in the background.

Opposite bottom: A view from Pratt of the Sanitary District Canal, along the western boundary of West Ridge, under construction in 1910.

Top: The Birchwood Country Club (BCC), a few years after it was built in 1906, was located at Chase (later 1217 W.) at the lake. A golf course was operated for a number of years north of Howard Street.

because the hospital was not accepting them at that time. The new hospital was built at a cost of $126,000, and in the 1960s, the land was used to construct the Howard-Western shopping center, while the hospital building later became Bethesda Hospital.

Birchwood and the Country Club

As Rogers Park continued to grow after the turn of the century, there was also activity in Birchwood, the section of the neighborhood along the lake north of Touhy and south of Germania. It would have a small business dis-

trict develop around the L stop at Jarvis that was opened in 1908.

The number of residents living in Birchwood was expanding and the real estate firm of Reeves and Beebe, one of the developers of the area, agreed to set aside forty feet along Lake Michigan between Chase and Sherwin that could be used for neighborhood recreation. A group of Birchwood residents opened the Birchwood Country Club on July 4, 1906, with membership in the Club limited to one hundred individuals who were supposed to live in Birchwood.

Top and bottom: A sunrise over Lake Michigan as seen from the porch of the Birchwood Country Club around 1915. The Arts & Crafts style furniture and railing in this scene were in vogue during this period. The Club was established in the 1890s and existed until 1942 when the property was sold to the North Shore School. Since the Club did not own the water rights, the land was purchased by a developer. Landfill was used as part of the construction of a three-story thirty-six unit apartment building erected immediately east. This new structure blocked the Club's lake access and these views.

ON SHERIDAN ROAD BEFORE LEAVING SATURDAY MORNING

First Auto Run of the
BIRCHWOOD COUNTRY CLUB
Aug. 7th & 8th 1915
TO STARVED ROCK, ILL.
20 CLUB CARS – 101 MEMBERS

The activities of the club were devoted to lectures, musical programs and dramatics. At one time George Ade and John McCutcheon wrote a sketch called "Birch Center" and Maude Wright of Hinsdale came and dramatized it and different members of the club took the parts...For ten years after its organization the club formed part of the life of the community and had increased its membership to 250.
History of Rogers Park, Document #43, Henry Howenstein

Construction in the Birchwood section of Rogers Park included a house designed in 1915 by the famous architect, Frank Lloyd Wright. The house was built at 7415 N. Sheridan for Emil Bach, co-owner of the Bach Brick Company. When his brother, Otto, purchased Wright's 1908 Oscar Steffen residence at 7631 N. Sheridan, he persuaded Emil to live nearby in a Wright-designed house of his own. The Bach homes were the first of a series of houses and apartment buildings in the Birchwood neighborhood. The Emil Bach house has survived into the twenty-first century.

Members of the Birchwood Country Club line up on Sheridan Road north of Touhy for their First Auto Run to Starved Rock, Illinois. The run occurred on August 7th & 8th of 1915. The McKay, Uhl and Hurd homes, shown in the background, were on the west side of Sheridan Road and listed in the Book of the North Shore in 1910.

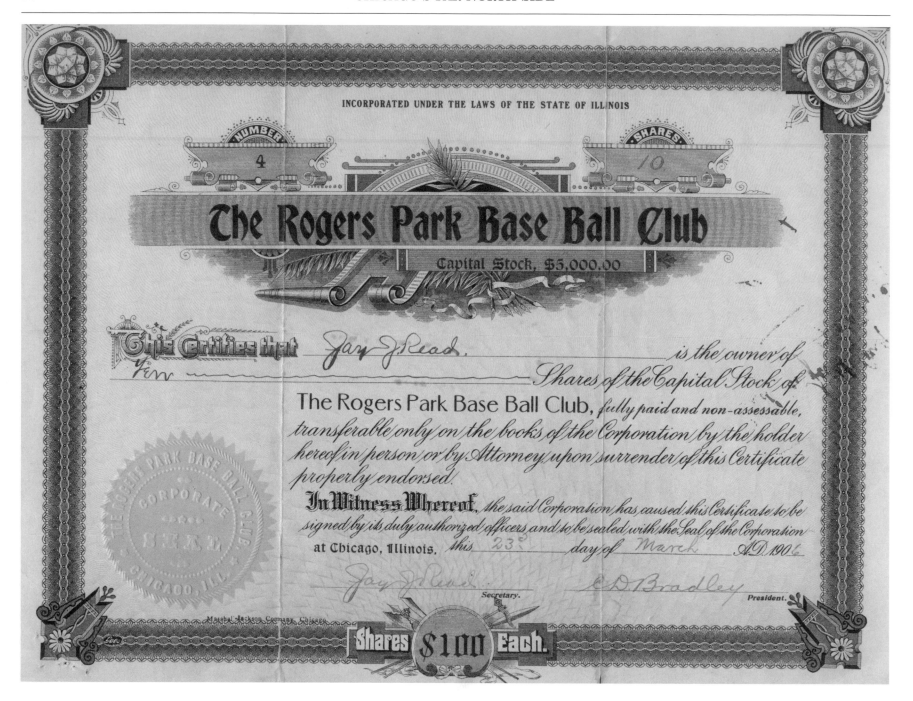

Opposite: Rogers Park Base Ball Club stock certificate issued in 1906 for ten shares of stock at $100 per share. The total amount of stock sold for the club was $5,000 or 50 shares.

Top and bottom: The Rogers Park Base Ball Grounds, near Devon and Clark, was a popular place in 1906 for people of all ages. Streetcar employees, who worked at the nearby carbarns, had their own baseball team called "The Limits" that played at this field. The ball park operated for only ten years.

Germania and the Howard Street District

After annexation of Rogers Park and West Ridge 1893, there was also an interest in convincing Chicago to annex the section named Germania (so-called because of its many German residents), once known as "no-man's land," to the northern border of Rogers Park. The primary supporters of annexation were the developers of the area: Charles W. Ferguson, Denis F. Ryan, Ben Lowenmeyer, A. L. Loangille and Seward Gunderson. This area was located between Rogers Park and South Evanston. Since Evanston had been unable to provide basic services to the subdivision, Germania seceded from Evanston in 1912. Three years later, Evanston passed an ordinance that allowed Germania to be annexed to Chicago. In the spring of 1915, despite opposition from some Chicago aldermen who didn't want to annex a "dry" area into the city, Chicago's Mayor Harrison signed an ordinance passed by the City Council that annexed Germania to Chicago, thus expanding Rogers Park's northern boundary. In the decade prior to the annexation, Charles W. Ferguson, a land developer, had bought large parcels of land from farmers and then sold sections to builders.

Opposite: The Emil Bach House, at 7415 N. Sheridan, was designed by Prairie School architect, Frank Lloyd Wright and built in 1915. The Bach home was designated a Chicago landmark in September 1977.

Right: Orwig's Map of Rogers Park includes the Germania district prior to its annexation to Chicago in May of 1915. Harry I. Orwig was a surveyor and civil engineer for Rogers Park and the North Shore.

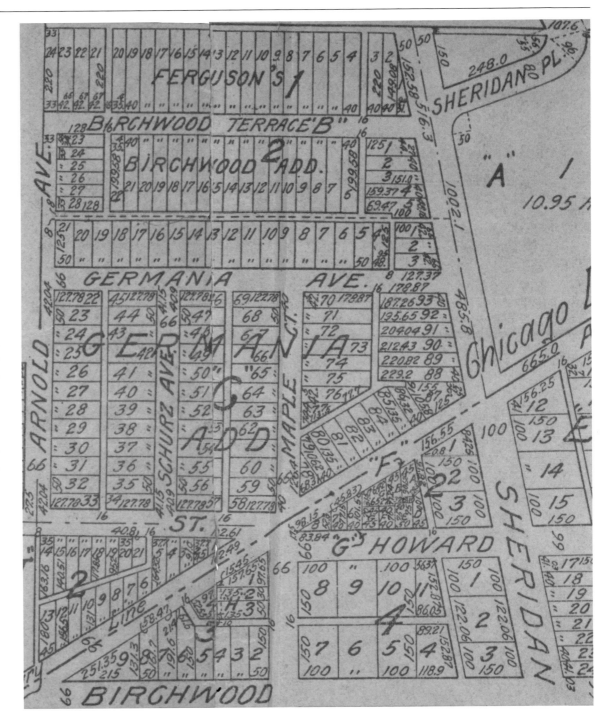

HOWARD Avenue is World-Famous as the Street of Fortune. This is the Last Opportunity to Buy in this Wonder District, before values take another startling increase.

In 1913, Ferguson sold the corner of Howard and Paulina to Denis F. Ryan for $18,000. Ryan was able to sell the land in 1925 to the United Cigar Stores for $350,000. In another similar deal, Ferguson sold land at Howard and Ashland for $1,800 that was bought in the 1920s by Kresge's Drug Store for $70,000. **Northside Sunday Citizen, December 30, 1927**

Before 1892 the area around what is now Howard Street was practically all wild prairie and woods. Farmers by the name of O'Leary, Bugner, and Keyes owned most of the land. In 1892 the Germania

subdivision…was divided into lots and sold to settlers who came with the purpose of making houses there. They did not succeed, however, because they could get no city improvements such as sewers, lights, a school and so forth. Most of them had to sell out; some merely abandoned their land…In 1910, I became interested in the district and bought quite a lot of land. The reason I thought the area could be something was because it was a center of transportation in a local sense. The Northwestern Elevated had a station at Howard Street and the Chicago streetcars came to Howard at Clark Street. **History of Rogers Park, Document #65, Charles W. Ferguson**

The section now called Howard District was in those days but a strip of forest called "No Man's Land"…early pioneer settlers were Pratt, Richards, Murphy, P. Philip, Muno, Zender, Devine, Weimeskirch, Reynolds, Clark, Gardner, Thorogood, Schreiber, Ure, and F. H. Doland…Early issues of the Rogers Park News *depict the deplorable condition of streets and pavements, the unlighted districts and the laborious progress of horsecars drawn by nags of skin and bones. Despite these handicaps, the first land boom commenced.* **North Shore News, October 11, 1940**

HOWARD THEATRE BUILDING · EXPRESS STATION NORTHWESTERN "L" CHICAGO

HENRY L. NEWHOUSE
ARCHITECT
CHARLES W. FERGUSON
OWNER

After Germania's annexation to Chicago, Charles Ferguson began the process of developing the area that would eventually be named after the son of one of the early farmers, John F. Ure. Ure was born in 1869 and lived on a farm between Rogers and Birchwood, east of Clark. When he donated the right-of-way on Howard to the city in 1897, he named the street for his son, Howard Ure.

Howard Street became a transportation hub with the opening of the Howard Street L stop in 1908 in combination with the Chicago and Northwestern train station and the terminal for Clark Street surface lines. These led to the subsequent apartment, theater, and café construction boom in the area around Howard. During the 1920s and 1930s the area became one of the liveliest entertainment centers on Chicago's North Side.

One of the earliest buildings constructed on Howard Street in 1918, and located on the former Ure farm, was the Howard Theatre, one of Chicago's movie house palaces.

About 1915, Charles W. Ferguson, a real estate man, built a business block containing some dozen stores and a movie on Howard Street. This was looked upon as a very dubious business proposition. About the same time the Burton Holmes Laboratories were constructed back of the business block containing the movie. **History of Rogers Park, Document #64, Student Paper**

After World War I, during the 1920s, the Howard and Birchwood areas of Rogers Park would become part of one of Chicago's biggest booms in real estate construction.

Opposite: A real estate ad to secure business frontage at ground floor prices in the new Howard Avenue District around 1915.

Above: The Howard Theatre Building was constructed in 1918 by Charles W. Ferguson at the onset of the development of the Howard Avenue Business District.

Opposite top left: Kenilworth Avenue (now Touhy) looking east toward Sheridan Road around 1910.

Opposite top right: Looking east on Devon from Newgard in the early 1900s.

Opposite bottom left: Looking west on Morse from Greenview in the early 1900s. This scene shows some of the first houses, with birch trees in the front yards.

Opposite bottom right: Looking north along the east side of Ridge Avenue north of Touhy in 1900.

Left: Cadets lead a parade of new recruits down Lunt Avenue to Northwestern station in 1917.

Devon Av. E from Newgart, Chicago, Ill.

MORSE AV. W. OF GREENVIEW.
ROGERS PARK, CHICAGO, ILL.

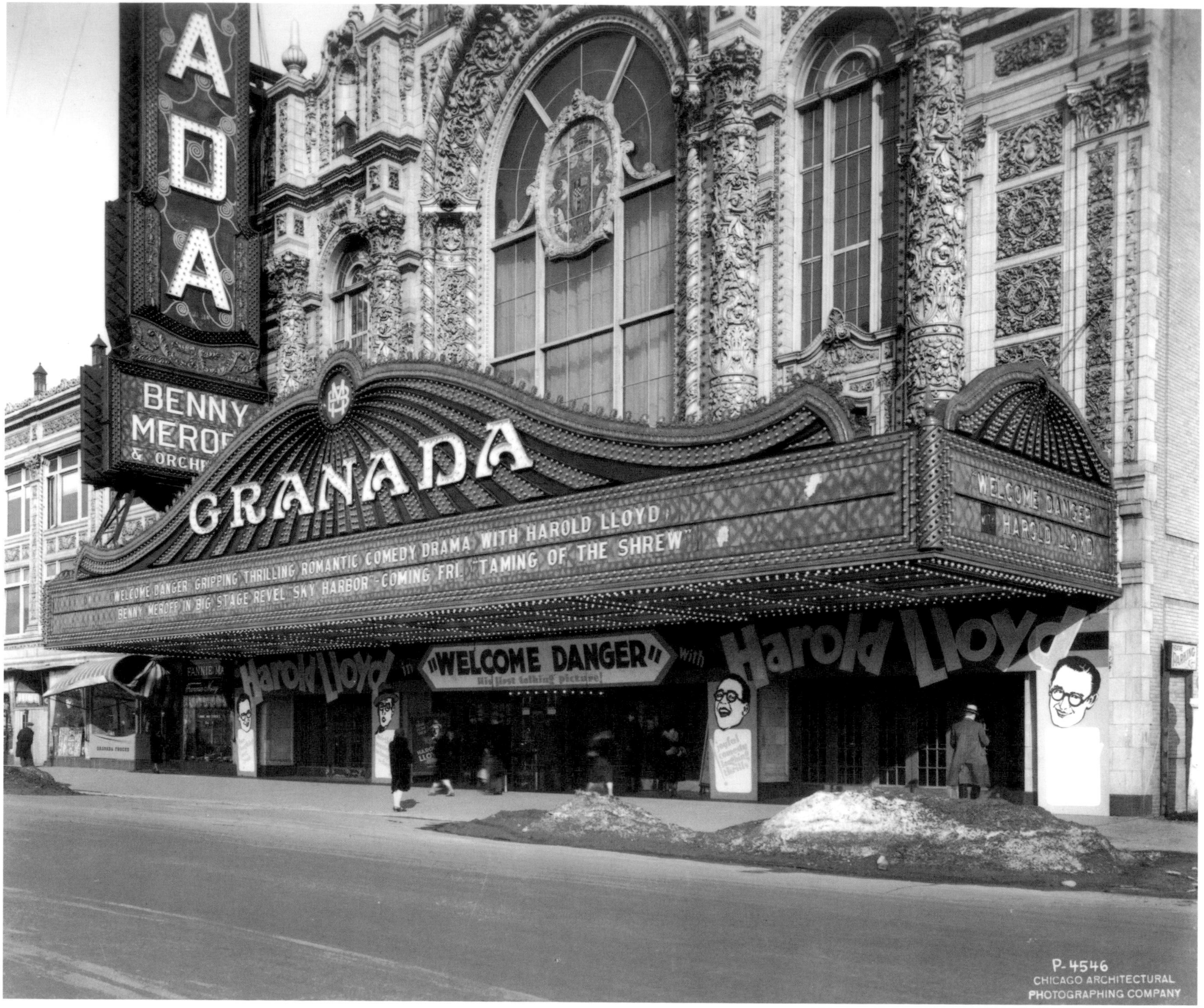
ADA
BENNY
GRANADA
WELCOME DANGER GRIPPING THRILLING ROMANTIC COMEDY DRAMA WITH HAROLD LLOYD
BENNY MEROFF IN BIG STAGE REVEL "SKY HARBOR" - COMING FRI. "TAMING OF THE SHREW"
"WELCOME DANGER"
HAROLD LLOYD
Harold Lloyd
in
"WELCOME DANGER"
His first talking picture!
with
Harold Lloyd
P-4546
CHICAGO ARCHITECTURAL
PHOTOGRAPHING COMPANY

THE BUILDING BOOM
1920 - 1930

The annexation and planned development of Germania, the expansion of the Northwestern elevated line from Wilson Avenue to Evanston, the construction of new buildings near the Edgewater Golf Club, and the economic boom that followed World War I, all led to the greatest period of growth in Rogers Park and West Ridge. From 1919 until 1930, the population of Chicago's Far North Side exploded as the construction of new apartment buildings and hotels, businesses, churches, synagogues, and movie theaters continued at a frenetic pace. While the population of the neighborhoods totaled 10,000 residents in 1914, Rogers Park and West Ridge increased to more than 96,000 by the end of the 1920s.

During the 1920s, Rogers Park and West Ridge experienced a building boom that was not matched for the next eighty years. Two- and three-story courtyard and multi-apartment buildings, apartment hotels, theaters, and a variety of new businesses appeared throughout both neighborhoods with the focus of construction on several specific locations. These included the Germania/Howard/Birchwood district, Sheridan Road from Devon Avenue to Touhy Avenue and west to Clark Street, the area south of Pratt Boulevard and west of Western Avenue (attracted by the Edgewater Golf Club relocation to Pratt and Ridge Boulevard) and the area surrounding Indian Boundary Park from Western to California Avenue.

West Ridge developed phenomenally after World War I and by 1930 the community had reached residential maturity. The area east of California Avenue was the site of most of the early residential construction in the 1920s... Most of the construction, however, was of brick bungalows and duplexes which soon supplanted the older one-family dwellings but also some two-flats and apartment buildings. West of California Avenue there were few improvements and less development and most of the northern section of West Ridge re-

$140,000.00
Greenleaf Apartment Building

First Mortgage 6½% Real Estate Gold Bonds

Bonds in Denominations of $100, $500 and $1,000

1415-1435 Greenleaf Avenue, Chicago, Illinois.

MATURITIES

$3,500.00 maturing	June 1, 1923	$ 3,500.00 maturing	Dec. 1, 1925
3,500.00 "	Dec. 1, 1923	3,500.00 "	June 1, 1926
3,500.00 "	June 1, 1924	3,500.00 "	Dec. 1, 1926
3,500.00 "	Dec. 1, 1924	3,500.00 "	June 1, 1927
3,500.00 "	June 1, 1925	108,500.00 "	Dec. 1, 1927

TITLE Guaranteed by Chicago Title and Trust Company Guarantee policy.

PROPERTY—190 feet frontage, 172 feet deep, improved with three-story brick building, containing six 5-room apartments, thirty 4-room apartments and one 4-room apartment and office in English basement. Also three-room apartment for janitor. Total thirty-eight apartments and one office.

VALUE Ground and Building, $230,000.00.

Bonds Owned and Offered for Sale at Par and Interest by the

Phillip State Bank and Trust Company
Northeast Corner of Clark Street and Lunt Ave.
CHICAGO, ILL.

Left: Phillip State Bank advertisement from 1929 for new apartment building at 1415-1433 West Greenleaf.

Examples of Rogers Park apartment buildings constructed during 1920s housing boom.

Opposite top left: Pratt and Lakewood, southwest corner.

Opposite top right: Pratt and Sheridan, southeast corner.

Opposite bottom left: 1357-67 West Greenleaf.

Opposite bottom right: Juneway and Paulina, southeast corner.

APTS. S.W. COR. LAKEWOOD AV. & PRATT BLVD.
ROGERS PARK, CHICAGO, ILL.
1246 B

APTS. S.E. COR. PAULINA ST.
& JUNE WAY TER. CHICAGO.

Apts. 1357-67 Greenleaf Av.
Rogers Park. Chicago.

APTS. S.E. COR. PAULINA ST.
& JUNE WAY TER. CHICAGO.

Opposite: Sherwin on the Lake, built in 1929, offered a resort atmosphere to the many people who stayed there over the years. It had its own beach, pier and taxi run to downtown Chicago.

Top left: Lincoln Apartments at Lunt and Paulina on the northeast corner.

Top right: Kenilworth Arms Apartments at Touhy and Paulina on the northwest corner.

Bottom: Millar Apartments at 6921-31 N. Greenview.

*mained undeveloped. Transportation for West Ridge residents improved with the extension of the Devon Avenue cable car line from Western Avenue to Kedzie Avenue in 1925. **Local Community Fact Book, Chicago Metropolitan Area, 1984, p. 4***

Construction of new, multi-unit apartment buildings began in the early 1920s along Estes, Touhy (Kenilworth) and Glenwood Avenues by the firm of Plotke and Grosby. A fifty-seven-unit apartment building, designed by architect Paul Olson, was built at the southwest corner of Jonquil Terrace and Hermitage at a cost of $500,000. Another $500,000 building was constructed at the southwest corner of Estes and Glenwood, known as the Glenshire Arms.

Work began April 15, 1922 on the Broadmoor Hotel located at the northwest corner of Howard Street and Bosworth Avenue. The six-story hotel cost $800,000 to build and contained ninety apartments and seven stores. It had a Roman classic front door and terra cotta trim and ornamentation on the front windows and doors. Built by Louis J. Rubin and N. D. Marks, the hotel became the home of a new radio station, WBBM-AM ("We Broadcast Broadmoor Music") which broadcast from this location for two years. Brothers, H. Leslie and Ralph Atlass began the radio station in the basement of their house in Lincoln, Illinois. The family then moved to a new home in Rogers Park at 7421 N. Sheridan, where they continued to operate the station before moving it to the Broadmoor. The new station began broadcasting on June 24, 1925, and using a new transmitter, located at

The Rogers Park Sand and Gravel Company supplied many of the building materials needed during the 1920s building boom.

PHONE BUCKINGHAM 5924

ROGERS PARK WASHED SAND
AND GRAVEL COMPANY

NOT INC.

2510 TOUHY AVENUE

JOSEPH J. MUNO   CHICAGO

the top of the hotel, aired such famous radio shows as "Amos and Andy" and "Fibber McGee and Molly," as well as live big band and jazz music.

The construction of apartment buildings in Rogers Park and the old Germania addition is proceeding at a rate that leaves one dizzy. Buildings containing nearly 1,600 high-grade apartments are now under way north of Estes Avenue and east of Clark Street...Howard Street boosters believe that the street is destined to develop rapidly. They point out that it has the advantage of a triple terminal -- the Clark Street surface lines and the Northwestern and Evanston elevated railways -- and that the section is rapidly being built up three and four stories high with apartments that attract a high-class tenancy. Good transportation, nearness to the Lake, quiet and freedom from dust, dirt and smoke combine to make the district one of the most attractive residential sections of the city. **Harry Beardsley, <u>Chicago Daily News</u>, 1922**

In addition to rapid construction of new apartment buildings in Rogers Park, a group of large, cooperative apartment buildings was also developed in West Ridge, surrounding the new Indian Boundary Park. The Park Gables was completed in 1928. Designed by James Denson, it was located on the north side of the park, on Estes west of Western. Denson also designed the Park Castles, Park Manor and Park Crest on the east side of the park.

Top: The North Shore Holder, on Kedzie near North Shore, was built in 1926 by the Peoples Gas, Light and Coke Company.

Bottom: The interior of the Holder's equipment building.

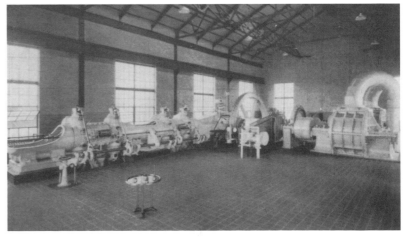

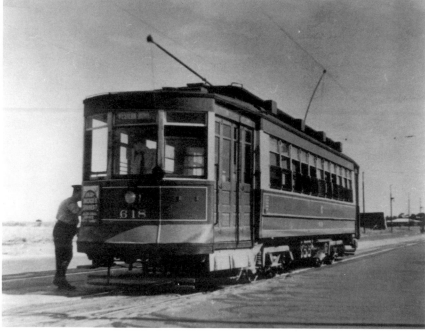

Top left: The Devon Avenue double-decker bus began its route on Devon and traveled to downtown Chicago via Sheridan Road and Lake Shore Drive. The Chicago Motor Bus Company began service in 1917 with gasoline-powered buses. It later merged with the Chicago Motor Coach Company. The company was forced to sell its assets to the Chicago Transit Authority in 1952.

Top right: A Western Avenue streetcar in 1921 heads south from Howard Street.

Bottom left: The Devon Car House, located at 6454-64 N. Clark Street, was built by the Chicago Union Traction Company and opened in 1901. It became a depot for several North Side streetcar routes. This building, shown in 1930, extended nearly two full blocks. This carbarn/depot closed in 1957 when the CTA converted the last north side streetcar route to buses. The 24th Police District is now located on this site.

Opposite: The reconstruction of the Devon Avenue Car House in 1923. A major fire in 1922 destroyed ninety wooden streetcars, but the Chicago Surface Lines, the world's largest streetcar operator, had all of the lines from the barn running the next day.

RAVENSWOOD AV

DEVON AV. CAR HOU
REAR
6-13-1923.

The new cooperative apartments at the Indian Boundary Park are selling from $6,000 to $12,000 an apartment, and they are reported to be selling rapidly too. They are very splendid appearing apartments with a fine setting right on the edge of the park, as though that were their front yard.
The Lincolnite, December 17, 1925

Construction of the Beachton Court Apartments began in 1928 at the southwest corner of Pratt and Ashland Avenue. Built at a cost of $350,000 and designed by Leon F. Urbain, it was a high-grade, fireproof apartment building with reinforced concrete construction. The six-story courtyard building, with seventy-six apartments, was designed in the Modern Tudor Gothic style of architecture.

Throughout Rogers Park and West Ridge, apartment buildings constructed during the 1920s also included commercial space or storefronts on the street level. These buildings could be found on major thoroughfares such as Devon, Pratt, Morse, Howard, Sheridan and Ridge. One of these buildings, on the southeast corner of Howard and Ridge, was built in 1926 at a cost of $126,000. The building housed a dress shop, men's clothing store, beauty shop and pharmacy on the street level.

Life in the 1920s

During the 1920s, the Rogers Park beaches along Lake Michigan were a very popular attraction for neighborhood residents. The beaches stretched from Loyola University on the south to Juneway Terrace on the north. The most popular locations along the lake were

at Farwell, Morse, Lunt, Greenleaf, Estes and Touhy. Their park-like settings, recreational equipment, refreshment stands and picnic tables made them ideal locations for area residents to escape the summer heat.

In the evenings, the horse-drawn so called "waffle wagons" took over. Very picturesque, especially after dark, as lanterns illuminated the interiors, showing the stock, with the proprietor busy popping popcorn over a gas flame in the front part

Opposite: Scene looking northwest shows Indian Boundary Park and the apartment buildings that surround it — on the east the Park Crest (1925), the Park Manor (1926), the Park Castles (1927) and on the north, the Park Gables (1929).

Above: Photographer takes pictures at Morse Avenue Beach, 1929. Chicago Historical Society: DN-088419-Chicago Daily News.

SCENE ON THE BEACH.
ROGERS PARK. CHICAGO, ILL. 2237 B

Opposite top: Beach at Estes Avenue looking north toward Lifeguard Station at Touhy. The Birchwood Country Club is visible just north on the shoreline.

Opposite bottom: View of Estes Beach in the 1920s showing the diving platform in the lake.

Above: Postcard scene of Touhy Beach looking south toward Farwell pier, c. 1920.

of the wagon. They also sold candy bars, gum, peanuts, pop, hot dogs, coffee and the like. The best seller was the Bunte "Tango Bar." They moved from street end to street end and found time to deviate from their rounds to serve the crowds at any of the softball games. **Norm Coughlin, "The Way It Was," Rogers Park Historical Society Newsletter, Summer, 1986**

Opposite: A view of Howard Street looking west toward Ashland shows the Cuneo Building on the southwest corner. Chicago Historical Society: ICHi-25860.

Top: This 1920s view shows Ullrich's Restaurant on the east side of Clark south of Howard. The streetcar turnaround was located just north of the restaurant.

Bottom: The Rogers Park Post Office, located on Paulina north of Howard, is shown c. 1930. Chicago Historical Society: ICHi-DN-094214-Chicago Daily News.

The Howard District Business Association was very active in the continuing development of Howard Street. The Association was influential in widening Paulina and in the annexation of a strip of Sheridan Road (from Rogers Avenue to Calvary Cemetery) to Chicago in 1926. The Association was also responsible for improving police protection in the area, a new lighting system in 1925, development of the Howard Beach, and creation of a Howard Street train station served by the Chicago and Northwestern Railway. The increase in population in the area also led to the completion of a new public elementary school, the Stephen Francis Gale School, on September 4, 1922, at 1631 W. Jonquil.

On September 18, 1926, the Granada Theatre, one of the grandest palace theaters in Chicago, opened. Located on Sheridan just north of Devon, the theater was built on the site of the original St. Ignatius Church. The Granada seated over 3,400 patrons and its beauty was enhanced by a six-story baroque facade adorned with a lavish variety of terra cotta and glass, thousands of lights on a ninety-three-foot marquee and French oak and glass doors at its entrance. The three-story, 190-foot long

Opposite: A night view of the Granada Theatre in 1926.

Left: Motorcycle policeman in front of North Shore Park District office at 1111 Farwell in 1928.

building included adjoining one-story commercial structures.

The architect of the Granada was Edward Eichenbaum of Levy and Klein, the architectural firm that also designed the Marbro, Regal and Diversey Theaters in Chicago. The Marks Brothers theatrical chain originally managed the Granada, but after the Great Depression of the 1930s, it was sold to Balaban and Katz, a well-known theater chain.

The theatre building included six adjacent stores, built as part of the original structure. Eventually, the entire block of Sheridan from Devon to the Loyola elevated train station housed eighteen stores. In the early years of operation, theater patrons were often treated to newsreel documentaries, vaudeville comedy acts, and performances by major stars such as Charlie Chaplin and Sophie Tucker, along with the presentation of the movie of the day.

Several other theaters opened in Rogers Park during the 1910s and 1920s. The North Shore Theatre on Sheridan Road near Albion was constructed in 1912. The Regent Theatre, later The 400 and currently the Village North, was located on Sheridan south of Pratt. The Howard Theatre Building was built in 1918 on Howard Street just east of the elevated station and further west was the Norshore Theatre (also part of the Balaban and Katz chain). The Adelphi Theatre opened in 1917 on Clark south of Estes. The Casino and the Park (also opened in 1912 on Clark) closed their doors in the 1920s because of competition from the nearby Adelphi.

Left: Construction began on the Nortown Theatre in 1930 and was completed the following year. Theatre Historical Society of America, Elmhurst, IL

Opposite: The Adelphi Theatre opened in 1917 on Clark south of Estes. This photograph was taken in the early 1950s. Theatre Historical Society of America, Elmhurst, IL

Opposite: Howard Theatre orchestra pit, c. 1920.

Right: The Thillens greenhouse, shown in the mid 1920s, was located at 2136 W. Peterson Avenue. The property bordered the Rosehill Cemetery Annex.

Now we move to Devon Avenue, turn left a few stores and view the medium large, modern Ellentee (sic) Theatre at 1550, constructed during World War One and ready to open on the plot of land that had once grown vegetables for Mr. Holleson. It, too, became a good neighborhood theatre for many decades. Later its name was changed to "The Ridge." **Norm Coughlin, "Old Rogers Park Moving Picture Theaters,"** <u>**Rogers Park Historical Society Newsletter**</u>**, Summer, 1988**

In 1925, streetcar service was expanded westward on Devon from Western to Kedzie and new tracks were added. The Devon Avenue extension provided area residents and merchants with an important means of transportation to housing and businesses.

Land does not seem to be particularly cheap. Streets where all the improvements are located sell for $125 a foot and up, more on the corners. Where the streets are not improved it runs around $80 a foot and up. The corner of Devon and Western, southeast, sold in 1911 for $4,500 and fifteen months ago was sold again for $200,000. A bank and possibly a movie theater will go in at or near this corner. **<u>History of West Rogers Park</u>, Document # 23, Walter Prigge**

Cor. Devon & Western Ave. Looking North July 12th 1923

A series of pictures taken from the intersection of Devon and Western on July 12, 1923. Real estate speculator signs can be seen as an indication of the beginnings of the building boom.

Opposite top: Devon & Western looking north.

Opposite bottom: Devon & Western looking south.

Top: Devon & Western looking east.

Bottom: Devon & Western looking west.

Top: A view of Devon and Western looking toward the southeast corner in 1934. The streetcar safety island can be seen in the foreground.

Bottom: A view of Devon and Western looking toward the northwest corner in 1934. Ben Bey Candies was located on this corner.

Top: Thiry's Household Utilities Corp., 1348 W. Devon, was one of the first electric shops in the area. It operated from 1920 until the early 1930s. The windows are filled with some of the latest appliances.

Bottom: An interior view of Thiry's Household Utilities in 1925 shows various electrical appliances. The shop also had a music department as indicated by the sheet music, guitar, victrola (windup record player) and listening booths.

Left: View of the construction of Mundelein College in 1930. Loyola University campus can be seen in the background.

Opposite top: The completed Mundelein College for Women as shown in a circa 1930 postcard. The college opened on September 28, 1930.

Opposite bottom: A Loyola Academy class picture in 1927.

Education in Rogers Park and West Ridge

As the population of Rogers Park continued its rapid growth, there was a need for more public schools. In the spring of 1926, students in the two upper-grade classes of Field and Gale (as well as Hayt and Swift schools located in Edgewater) were moved to a new red brick and white stone school at Albion and Bosworth known as Sullivan Junior High School. Its first nineteen graduates completed their high school education at Senn High School at Peterson Avenue and Clark. In 1930, the junior high school was renamed Sullivan High School.

During the 1920s, parochial grammar school education was available at St. Ignatius and St. Jerome and high school education at Loyola Academy and St. Scholastica. Loyola University in Rogers Park offered residents a college education.

On November 1, 1929, ground was broken for a new college located next to Loyola University. Mundelein College, a Catholic women's college, opened at 6363 N. Sheridan Road on September 28, 1930. Mundelein's main building, the first college skyscraper in the United States, was a triumph of art deco architecture. The college had been founded at George Cardinal Mundelein's request and was planned by Mother Mary Isabella, superior general of the Congregation of Sisters of Charity of the Blessed Virgin Mary. Known as the "college under one roof," there were four hundred women in its new student body in 1930.

The Growth of Rogers Park Religious Institutions

To meet the religious needs of the rapidly growing population of Rogers Park and West Ridge, there was a boom in the building of new churches and synagogues during the 1920s.

In 1919 Baptists moved into their new church which had been completed at 1900 W. Greenleaf...Among the massive churches constructed in the neighborhood were St. Paul By the Lake (1926), 7100 N. Ashland; Temple Mizpah (1924), 1615 W. Morse; Rogers Park Congregational Church (1927), 1545 W. Morse; B'nai Zion (1928), 1439 W. Pratt; and the Sixteenth Church of Christ Scientist (1929), at 7201 N. Ashland. **Pacyga and Skerrett, _Chicago: City of Neighborhoods_, p. 134**

The Rogers Park Baptist Church was organized in 1891 by a small group of residents. Originally worshipping at Greenleaf and Paulina, a new building at Greenleaf and Wolcott was dedicated in 1919.

In 1893, St. Mary's Church of Evanston established a mission in Rogers Park, and by 1894, the new congregation, renamed St. Jerome, had built a small church at the northwest corner of Morse and Paulina. A larger church was erected at Lunt and Paulina in 1916. St. Ignatius was established in 1907 on the east side of Sheridan, north of Devon. The parish moved to a new structure at 6559 N. Glenwood in 1917. St. Jerome and St. Ignatius were the two Roman Catholic parishes in the area.

Left: St. Henry Church, built in 1905, was the third and last built by the parishioners. Located on the southwest corner of Devon and Ridge, it was later used by Angel Guardian Orphanage and now by the Croatian Catholic Church.

Top: The Rogers Park Baptist Church, dedicated in 1919, is located at Greenleaf and Wolcott on the northwest corner.

Bottom: The Rogers Park Methodist Episcopal Church was located at Greenleaf and Ashland on the northwest corner. A fire destroyed this structure in 1968 and its members combined with the Rogers Park Congregational Church to become the United Church of Rogers Park.

In 1874, the Methodist Episcopal Church was located in Rogers Park on Greenleaf Avenue, west of Clark. In 1886, the Episcopalians opened St. Paul's Mission at Lunt and Paulina, and, in 1926, the St. Paul's-by-the-Lake congregation moved to its new site at 7100 N. Ashland. The First Congregational Church of Rogers Park erected its first building in the neighborhood in 1889 at 1701 W. Morse, but by 1906, needed a larger site and a building was constructed at the southeast corner of Morse and Ashland.

Other churches included the Rogers Park Presbyterian Church at 7059 N. Greenview (built in 1910) and the Sixteenth Church of Christ Scientist at the northeast corner of Touhy and Ashland (built in 1929).

The Howard Community Church began in 1917 as a mission of the Rogers Park Congregational Church and held services in a school building on Birchwood, later using commercial space on Howard near Ashland.

Bethesda Evangelical Lutheran Church was organized in West Ridge in 1920 and met in a storefront on Western north of Estes. As the congregation grew, it was able to purchase lots on Farwell and Campbell in 1923 and build a permanent building there in 1925.

The Jewish population of Rogers Park increased in the 1920s due to a major influx of second- and third-generation Russian and Hungarian Jews who moved north from their original locations on the West, Northwest and South Sides of Chicago. They began to migrate to Rogers Park when the elevated line was extended from Wilson to Howard in 1908, and with the building boom of the 1920s, their numbers on the Far North Side were increasing. Temple Mizpah and B'nai Zion, the first two synagogues established in Rogers Park, were formed between 1918 and 1919.

Temple Mizpah was the first Reform Jewish congregation on the North Side of Chicago. The building for the temple at 1615 W. Morse was dedicated in 1924. Until then, the members worshipped in the Masonic Hall on Lunt.

Temple Mizpah was founded in 1919, by a group of people in Rogers Park interested in Liberal or Reformed Judaism. From a small group of some twenty odd families it has grown to over five hundred. Acquiring the property on the corner of Morse and Ashland Boulevard, the Community House was erected in September of 1924...Rabbi Samuel S. Cohen was the first spiritual leader of the congregation, and Mr. David Labowitch is the president of the Organization from the time of inception. **History of Rogers Park, Document #67, Rabbi Singer**

B'nai Zion was founded in Rogers Park in 1918 as a Conservative Jewish congregation, and was organized by Herman Spivak, Edward Steiff and Joseph Friedman. The first services were held at the Odd Fellows Hall at the corner of Lunt and Clark. During the first year of existence membership totaled sixteen, but increased to eighty-five by 1921. With the increasing size of the congregation, a permanent structure was built at the southeast corner of Pratt and Greenview. The combined temple and school was dedicated September 8, 1928 and was presided over by Rabbi Abraham Lassen.

(B'nai Zion) was organized in August of 1918. Up to June 1919 we were located at 1715 Lunt Avenue. We bought our present site from St. Paul By the Lake, that is, the Lunt property...The church has been used for services until the present when we began using the Masonic Temple across the street from the church for office space and for social gatherings. In June 1924 we bought our present site at 1439 Pratt Boulevard...(In 1927) there are 275 families in good standing...Of the original eighteen families when I arrived, one from Holland, two from Hungary, three from Russia, the others being American...This is a lovely neighborhood of residences. The homes are stable. **History of Rogers Park, Document #69, Rabbi Lassen**

Growth in the 1920s followed by Disruption in the '30s and '40s

As the 1920s ended, Rogers Park and West Ridge had experienced one of the largest building booms and population expansions in the history of Chicago. Yet, for the next twenty years, its residents would have to cope with one of the most volatile periods in American history as worldwide economic depression and a Second World War would disrupt the lives of the neighborhoods.

Street scene on Ridge Avenue looking south from Pratt in the mid 1920s. At this time many greenhouses were located on the east side of Ridge.

THE DEPRESSION AND WWII
1931 - 1945

The Great Depression of the 1930s and World War II (1941-1945) had a significant effect on the daily lives of residents of Rogers Park and West Ridge, just as these events affected other Chicagoans and Americans across the country.

During the Depression, the total population of Rogers Park grew by only 3,500 (to a total of 60,500 residents in 1940). There was a ten-percent increase in the population of West Ridge (from 39,700 to 43,500) during the same period. The sharp drop in construction in both neighborhoods during the 1930s was not reversed until after the war.

*Commercial ventures were still few and scattered in West Ridge in 1930, although there were the beginnings of a business district on Western Avenue following the construction of a bank building. The greenhouses that flourished at the turn of the century were rapidly disappearing as residential development encroached upon them. Along the North Shore Channel from Touhy to Pratt avenues there were still some brick plants and a few factories. In 1929 a new post office was built at Devon and Talman Avenues and the use of the name "North Town" as an alternative to West Ridge dates from that year. **Local Community Fact Book, Chicago Metropolitan Area**

The residents of both neighborhoods struggled to pay for housing, food, entertainment and medical costs on reduced family incomes. Still they were generous to neighbors and others who also suffered during the worldwide economic crisis. The residents of Rogers Park and West Ridge patriotically supported the war effort in a variety of ways. Many joined the American armed forces, while others served as air raid wardens. They worked in war industries and supported the American Red Cross, U.S. Savings Bond drives, and initiatives to preserve vital resources like rubber, paper and aluminum. Residents used ration stamps to purchase groceries and gaso-

Opposite: Devon Avenue, looking west from Western in 1934.

Top: Western Avenue, looking north from Devon in 1934. The Historical Society's building, built in 1929-30, is seen in the distance on the left.

Bottom: Western Avenue, looking south from Devon in 1934. The Nortown Theatre, opened April 4, 1931, is seen in the distance.

Top: A Chicago Surface Line streetcar is seen on Devon Avenue, looking east from Western, c. 1940.

Bottom: View of Devon Avenue, looking west, toward Western in 1934.

line and planted Victory Gardens throughout the neighborhoods to provide fruits and vegetables for their families.

The 1930s

The 1920s building boom continued into the early 1930s, as new apartment buildings, theaters and stores were being completed, and before the Great Depression affected the area. Once the full force of the Depression was felt in the neighborhoods, residents in need received regular assistance from their neighbors.

A rummage sale will be held for the benefit of Rogers Park Relief station, 7067 N. Clark... An appeal is made to all residents of Rogers Park to donate furniture and clothing, which are salable, to the station...Rogers Park Catholic Women's Club and Woman's Neighborhood Club furnished helpers a (sic) the station last week... Dr. A. J. Kelley has offered to give medical attention to needy families referred to him by the station and S. M. Wayte of Ridge Pharmacy is filling prescriptions free of charge for those sent by the station. Food was donated by North Shore Vegetable Market, Campbell's Grocery and Fruit Market...Bread was donated by Davidson's Bakery, Burkland's Bakery, Morse Avenue Bakery and Anderson's Bakery...Other food was donated by Field School, Sullivan Junior High... **"Plan Rummage for Rogers Park Relief,"** <u>**The Howard News,**</u> **January 28, 1932**

The Depression directly affected the neighborhoods when, on June 21, 1932, the Phillip State Bank closed due to lack of funds. In 1895, it had been the first bank to open in Rogers Park and was a major source of financial support for area residents after the neighborhoods were annexed to Chicago. It wasn't until January 21,1941, that depositors of the defunct bank were told that they would be receiving a twelve and a half-percent dividend. This was a result of a suit won by the bank receiver's office in the Superior and Appellate Courts against the Cook County treasurer for bank funds that had been claimed by the treasurer.

Although the boom in construction of new movie houses peaked in the 1920s, theaters were busy during the 1930s as people sought affordable recreation during the Depression.

EMPLOYEES OF A. C. NIELSEN COMPANY
CHICAGO   DECEMBER 21, 1935

The Nortown Theatre opened on Western, south of Devon in April 1931. Rogers Park and West Ridge were no longer dry communities once Prohibition ended in 1933, and residents visited restaurants, taverns and nightclubs to celebrate this new freedom. Howard Street became a center of activity. Area residents, transients arriving by elevated train or bus, and students from Northwestern University frequented the taverns and nightclubs on the busy street at the north end of the city. One of the most popular venues was the "Limehouse," located at 1559 W. Howard. This restaurant operated from 1931 until 1954 and offered Cantonese dishes as well as dancing to the Duane Woodruff Orchestra and fashion shows that included a bridal display.

In 1935 Arthur C. Nielsen, Sr. moved the A. C. Nielsen Company into a new two-story building at 2101 W. Howard in Rogers Park. He had founded the company in 1923 at its first location in the Lake View area of Chicago.

The company started conducting inventories at food and drug stores, but is most famous for its "Ratings System", developed by Nielsen, and used by radio and TV stations and advertisers across the country.

By the 1950s, the company had grown to be the largest marketing research company in the world with offices in 20+ countries and the Howard Street address was its International Headquarters. Arthur C. Nielsen, Jr. joined the company in the 1940s, was its president and CEO for many years and continues to serve as a consultant to the business.

Opposite: A view of large commercial and apartment building at Howard and Marshfield, c. 1940.

Above: The original A. C. Nielsen Company headquarters at 2101 W. Howard in 1935.

Just below Calvary was a strip called for a time "No Man's Land," but afterward invaded by Everyman and his wife. This is the Howard Street district, which became a bright-light area with amazing speed. Roger (sic) Park, just south of it, hums with life and with wheels. It glows feverishly at one place, where stands a prodigious movie theater (the Granada), just back of which, in sharp contrast, lies a group of redbrick buildings clearly academic. This is the North Side headquarters of Loyola University, outgrowth of old St. Ignatius College. **Chicago: A Portrait, 1931, p. 216**

Opposite: The southern border of Rogers Park at the northeast corner of Devon and Sheridan. The Granada Theatre and the Mobil Oil station have both been replaced by apartment and office buildings, c. early 1940s.

Right: Gas station attendants, c. 1940, at station located south of the Granada Theatre.

Education in the Community

During the 1930s, there was need for more public elementary schools and the Joyce Kilmer Elementary School opened at 6700 N. Greenview (next to Sullivan Junior High School) on September 7, 1931. Later in the decade, Phillip Rogers Elementary School, the second public elementary school in West Ridge after Armstrong School, opened in 1937 at Jarvis and Washtenaw Avenues.

In 1938, the Dix family opened the North Shore School in Rogers Park with an initial enrollment of twenty-two students. It was a private K-8 school located in a mansion on the 7700 block of N. Sheridan. Mr. Dix was from Tennessee, while Mrs. Dix had lived in Kentucky. Both had backgrounds in fine arts, drama and music, as well as school administration and teaching. In 1943 the North Shore School bought and renovated the old Birchwood Country Club at 1217 W. Chase that had closed during the Depression.

Top: Boone School graduating class of January 1936.

Bottom: Sullivan High School cooking class, circa 1930.

Top: Rogers School 4th grade class, 1937.

Bottom: Kilmer Elementary School band, 1930.

Top: Aerial view of Loyola University and Mundelein College, c. 1940.

Bottom: Sullivan High School, looking south on Bosworth.

Opposite top: Temple Mizpah Confirmation class, 1938.

Opposite bottom: Gale School class, June 1934.

Sports in the Community

With the popularity of baseball, known as "America's pastime," a new baseball park was built by Mel Thillens in 1938. The park was located on the north side of Devon at Kedzie just east of the Sanitary District Canal. North Town Currency Stadium soon became one of the most popular entertainment venues in West Ridge, Rogers Park, and surrounding neighborhoods and suburbs. The field was soon renamed Thillens Stadium after its founder.

Mel was working as a bank clerk when the Depression hit and the bank closed. He then went to work at a currency ex-

change and shortly thereafter thwarted five bandits. After this episode, the owner sold the business to Mel and the Thillens Checashers was born. From the success of his business enterprise, in 1938 he was able to build the ballpark we now know at a cost of $75,000. The fences, bleacher seats, lights, the scoreboard and the concession stand were all installed. __***Rogers Park Historical Society Newsletter***__*__,__ **Summer, 1988**

In response to information from the Office of War that the major league baseball season might have to be suspended due to the shortage of manpower, a group of Chi-

cago baseball men discussed forming a women's league. Philip K. Wrigley, owner of the Chicago Cubs, and a group of his colleagues including Branch Rickey and Mel Thillens organized the All-American Girls Professional Baseball League (AAGPBL) in 1943.

Tryouts were held at Wrigley Field. Dress rules included short hair, jeans, short skirts, make-up and physical attractiveness. Women were chosen based on speed, power and competitive spirit. Games were played in Illinois, Indiana, Michigan and Wisconsin. The team sponsored by Thillens Checashers played at Thillens Stadium against many other teams until the league dissolved in 1954.

Opposite: View of night game between Blue Room and Regal at North Town stadium, August 27, 1945.

Top: Thillens North Town Stadium promotional truck advertising "major league" softball games.

Bottom: Postcard advertising "major league" softball games at North Town Currency Stadium in 1947.

Opposite: Two players prepare for a game as members of the All-American Girls' Professional Baseball League (AAGPBL) in 1943. The League became the basis for the 1992 film, "A League of Their Own."

Right: The foyer of the Chicago Town and Tennis Club, located at 1925 W. Thome, circa 1940. The building was later the local Elks Club and is now the Unity Church of Chicago.

FOYER
CHICAGO TOWN AND TENNIS CLUB

The 1940s

As war broke out in Europe and Asia in 1939, the United States found itself keenly interested in the outcome of the battles. Rogers Park and West Ridge residents were increasingly involved in war-related activities. In February 1941, the Rogers Park unit of the British War Relief Society received many offers of assistance. Several local stores donated shoes and clothing, while local churches and clubs formed groups in support of the war effort. Offers of clothing and bedding continued throughout 1941 and neighborhood residents demonstrated their concern for the British who came under daily attack from Germany.

Britain's most urgent civilian needs were outlined this week by Mrs. Henry Cambridge, 1245 Chase, chairman of the Rogers Park branch of the British War Relief Society...Articles needed include air-raid shelter equipment, woolen blankets and cots, sleeping bags, rubber air mattresses, mobile feeding kitchens, warm winter clothing for men, women and children, mackinaws, woolen under clothing, strong boots and shoes, woolen knitted goods, first aid equipment for rescue workers and ships, vegetable seeds, and asbestos gloves for civilian fire fighters. ***"British Aid Group Asks Funds, Goods,"*** <u>***Howard News***</u>***, March 18, 1941***

Even before the United States declared war, neighborhood residents were drafted or volunteered for service in various branches of the United States military. According to the <u>Howard News</u>, February 25, 1941: "Fifty five

*Opposite: The Rogers
Park American Legion
conducts a scrap drive
at Devon, Ashland and
Clark, c. 1942.*

*Top: Air Corp/U.S.
Army Recruiter's desk
at North Town Library,
c. 1941.*

*Bottom: Boy Scouts
participate in a
newspaper drive for the
Office of Civil Defense,
c. 1943. Chicago
Historical Society,
ICHi-22969.*

THE LIMEHOUSE

Full Course Dinner
85c and $1
Luncheon Fifty Cents
Sunday Dinner
$1 to $1.25

Dine and Dance

Briargate 0364

Jerry Potter Orchestra

1561 HOWARD STREET

No Cover Charge

Special
Entertainmen
Saturday
Evening

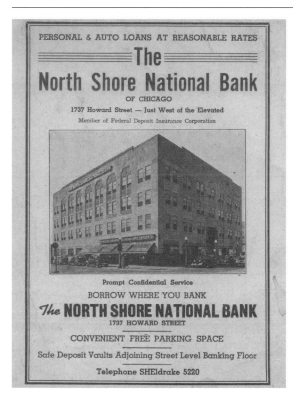

of the neighbors being inducted are volunteers. Board 75 at 6459 Sheridan is the only board with all volunteers and retains its record of entire volunteer induction to date. The March quota is expected to be greater than any thus far, with local boards furnishing from thirty to forty men each."

The attack by Japanese Imperial Armed Forces on December 7, 1941 and declarations of war on the United States and subsequently, United States declarations against Japan, Germany and Italy, brought the country into World War II. Residents of Rogers Park and West Ridge immediately responded to the crisis.

The Northside was put on a war basis Monday following Japan's sudden attack on Hawaii with two-man details on 24 hour duty assigned to guard Commonwealth Edison plants, telephone company offices, pumping stations, post offices, and Peoples Gas tanks. All leaves and time-off were cancelled for firemen and policemen. **"War Hits Northside," Rogers Park News, Tuesday, December 9, 1941**

Neighborhood residents stormed the joint office of civilian defense, war relief and USO at 1225 W. Devon to volunteer for mili-

Opposite: An advertisement for The Limehouse, 1561 W. Howard, c. 1940.

Above: Advertisements from a local Rogers Park newspaper, c. 1940.

tary duty. Young mothers, social workers, blood bank technicians and many others signed up for the war effort. Volunteers served as air raid wardens on each block in Rogers Park and West Ridge. The call went out for civilian defense workers to serve as fire wardens, auxiliary firemen and police, rescue squads, decontamination crews, nurses, cooks, time bomb volunteers and gas fighters.

There was a major push to save vital war materials such as paper, kitchen grease, aluminum, pant cuffs and other wool clippings, and tire rubber. Residents of the neighborhoods responded enthusiastically to the call for help. In West Ridge, Indian Boundary civilian defense (CD) workers held gas-defense training at Armstrong School. During May 1942, neighborhood residents attended an "I Am an American Day" held at Pottawattomie Park and watched Illinois Reserve Militia drill and demonstrate bayonet fighting. Over five hundred people attended an open house for the Sheridan-Devon CD center at 6507 N. Sheridan Road. That civilian defense office, under the elevated tracks, was one of the few semi-bomb proof buildings in Chicago.

The patriotic fervor also led citizens to turn in cameras, radios and guns that belonged to German refugees. They also reported neighbors of Japanese and Italian descent as "aliens," to area police stations.

Houses and apartment buildings were available for purchase in 1942, although there was limited movement by residents to new properties. Examples of housing costs included: 1806 W. Pratt -- a two-story frame residence containing six rooms and one bath with hot water heat plus a two-car frame garage, priced at $8,500 or at a rental of $55 per month;

Opposite: Frank Vitale's Shoe and Hat, located at Farwell and Clark, 1942.

Left: Della Frocks, an upscale dress store at 1640 W. Howard, 1940.

Left: Schaul's Poultry Farm, located on the northwest corner of Pratt and California in 1939. The Zimmer greenhouses can be seen in the background.

Opposite: Butcher shop in Rogers Park in 1936.

Opposite: North Town Check Cashing truck in 1945.

Right: A Bowman Dairy milk truck from 1941. The dairy was located at 1834 W. Columbia, on the current site of S&C Electric.

1613 W. Greenleaf -- a two-story frame residence containing eight rooms and one bath as well as a sleeping porch, with steam heat with oil burner and an automatic hot water heater, priced at $7,600; 1615 W. Columbia Avenue -- a three-story, forty-nine-unit apartment building, with twenty-four two-room and twenty-five three-room unfurnished apartments, priced at $85,000; and 7460 N. Ashland -- a three-story Birchwood apartment building with eighteen three- and four-room unfurnished apartments, priced at $38,000.

Neighborhood residents planted Victory Gardens to support the war effort by growing their own fruits and vegetables, thus allowing farmers to provide the necessary food for America's military and allied countries. In 1942 it was reported that forty-five Victory Gardens had been assigned to residents of the Fargo and Wolcott area of Rogers Park. In 1944, ground was broken for over two hundred new Victory Gardens located near Howard and Bell, Birchwood and Washtenaw, and Greenleaf and Ridge, which would accommodate over one hundred area families.

Unlike the job situation during the Depression, there were unlimited employment opportunities in the war years. A quick scan of the local newspapers in 1943 revealed the following: jobs for skilled workers building Douglas C-54 planes at the Douglas Aircraft Co. plant in Park Ridge; war work for tool makers, turret lathe operators and drill pressmen at the Barco Manufacturing Company at 1801 Winnemac Avenue; war work for men as punch press operators and girls as light machine and assembly workers at the Greenview Manufacturing Company at 2557 Greenview Avenue;

and light factory and machine work for girls and women at the Atlas Collapsible Tube Company at 1757 N. Kimball Avenue.

Daily life in the 1940s included the use of ration books to buy necessities. Businesses were watched closely by government agencies that monitored overcharging under the threat of being closed. One such incident occurred in September 1943 when a local meat market at 7007 N. Glenwood was forbidden by the Office of Price Administration (OPA) to sell rationed food for thirty days. The owner insisted he had not violated the pricing regulations, but the ruling remained.

Those on the home front dealt with the constant threat of being victimized by infantile paralysis, or polio, the disease that had struck President Franklin Delano Roosevelt. During the Labor Day weekend of 1943, there was a polio outbreak in Chicago. Officials identified twenty new cases on the North Side, which brought the total cases in Chicago that year to 492 with the death count at fifty. Polio would remain a health threat until the 1950s when Dr. Jonas Salk developed a vaccine that would eventually eliminate the disease.

As the war began to reach a critical point in 1944, a decision about land use was made that would have long-term implications for West Ridge. The focus was on the land along Kedzie, east of the Sanitary District Canal, between Touhy and Pratt.

The possibility that the huge West Rogers Park clay pit might be used as a dump without opposition by surrounding property owners appeared this week following a conference between officials of the West Rogers Park Property Owners association and the president of the Illinois Brick Company, which owns the pit. The property owners tentatively gave their approval to a plan that the pit be used for a dump under the "sanitary fill" method which has been the vogue in New York for many years and by which thousands of acres of land, including that upon which LaGuardia field now stands, have been reclaimed. **'Suggest Sanitary Fill for Clay Pit,' Rogers Park News, Thursday, February 24, 1944**

D Day, June 6, 1944, was a critical time and many residents of Rogers Park and West Ridge were concerned about the fate of their sons and daughters fighting in Europe and the Pacific. Local organizations such as the Rogers Park YMCA, at 6968 N. Clark Street, held regular meetings so that residents with loved ones missing in action or in enemy prison camps could share news and draw mutual comfort. With V-E Day in April 1945, and V-J Day in August of the same year, residents could grieve for the loss of relatives while breathing a sigh of relief. Peace had finally come after years of depression, war and great personal sacrifices.

Opposite: "Victory is not Peace" exhibit in the window of the Northtown Library c. 1945.

YEARS OF STABILITY
1946 - 1969

World War II was finally over, but its legacy dominated the nation. Americans mourned their dead and cared for their wounded, and many returning veterans sought to deal with the psychological impact of their wartime ordeals. A more tangible legacy of the war was the continuation of the serious wartime housing shortage (caused by the unavailability of construction workers and building materials for residential housing) and the shortage of essential consumer goods. The strong post-war economy, a dramatic contrast to the struggling economy of the pre-war years, would help the country overcome wartime shortages. A significant aspect of the legacy was a change in culture, roles and attitudes. New wartime roles for women and blacks reflected these changes. While there was movement back to traditional roles right after the war, gradual changes would soon appear, and there would be no turning back.

Hundreds of thousands of veterans returned to the United States in 1945 and 1946, launching a period of dynamic change. Families were reunited and others were started. There was a population boom and an explosion of residential construction. Schools were quickly stretched beyond capacity and the infrastructures couldn't keep up with ever-increasing demands. As business and industry made a transition to peacetime conditions, veterans, along with former defense plant workers, wondered what they would do in the face of an unsure job market. The nation would soon be involved in another war in Korea (which would be designated a police action). The Cold War, civil defense, McCarthyism and loyalty oaths would occupy people's attention. Polio would continue its dreaded presence until the disease was finally defeated.

The period started with the simplicity of soda fountains and bobby socks, corner drug stores and radio as the major source of information and entertainment. People shopped at "mom and pop" grocery stores, while children made up games and played in the street and peddlers rang bells to let housewives know they were there to sharpen knives and scissors. By the end of this period, simplicity would be replaced by *bigger, better, faster*. These changes, which were evident across the country, had a dramatic impact in Rogers Park and West Ridge.

The Communities in 1946

Though Rogers Park and West Ridge were adjoining communities, they were very different. Rogers Park was a more established neighborhood. A building boom in the 1920s covered most of the land with small businesses, apartment buildings and houses, including several of historical and architectural significance. The east side of the neighborhood was lined with beaches, which provided residents with clean and pleasant access to Lake Michigan. While much of Rogers Park was developed, the presence of vacant lots and small, undeveloped areas throughout the neighborhood provided places to build additional houses and apartments.

There were several shopping and commercial areas in Rogers Park. Clark Street, Devon Avenue, Howard Street and Sheridan Road had a variety of stores and restaurants, and there were smaller shopping and commercial areas located near the elevated train stations on Morse and Jarvis Avenues. Nightclubs and restaurants located on the east end of Howard Street attracted people from all areas of Chicago.

West Ridge had developed more slowly than Rogers Park, although the differences between West Ridge and Rogers Park were not evident in the eastern section, from Ridge Avenue to Western Avenue. This area was well built up with houses and apartment buildings. One block west of Western, along Lunt Avenue, was Indian Boundary Park, a showcase of the Chicago Parks system. The park housed the city's only zoo other than Lincoln Park. Indian Boundary Zoo had a lagoon that was the summer home to ducks

Opposite Top: Pratt looking east toward Sheridan in the late 1940s.

Opposite Bottom: East side of Ridge looking south from Albion in 1949.

Top: Cook County Federal Savings original location at 2326 W. Devon around 1948.

Bottom: Devon looking east at California in the mid 1940s. Randl's Restaurant later occupied this corner.

and geese, along with a wading pool for children. South of the park were several blocks of large, attractive houses which were comparable to the finest dwellings in Rogers Park.

However, in the mid-to late 1940s, the western part of West Ridge was sparsely developed. An area west of California Avenue and north of Pratt Boulevard, called Deere Park, was mostly prairie. Another portion of the neighborhood on its western boundary, Kedzie Avenue, was undeveloped, as was the northwest section, bordered by Western, Touhy, Kedzie and Howard. Most of this area was prairie, with scattered homes, some farms along Touhy, a few businesses on Western, and Philip Rogers Elementary School.

West Ridge had two commercial areas. Western had small stores and restaurants, as well as an art deco movie theater, the Nortown. Devon, between Western and California, was an upscale area where residents would shop, visit one of the numerous restaurants, see a movie at a Balaban and Katz theater or leisurely stroll. Though Devon was the most important commercial street in West Ridge, it was only partially developed in 1946. In this six-block area there still were several vacant lots. These lots would soon be developed to handle the shopping and business needs of thousands of new residents, while the strip of Devon west of California had few stores and buildings.

A Building Boom

The return of tens of thousands of veterans to the Chicago area intensified the already serious housing shortage. Due to the exten-

sion of wartime rent controls, apartments were scarce but affordable. Few new residential units were available as builders were just beginning to construct new houses and apartments after the war. It would take the building industry more than ten years to catch up with the demand. In addition, the price of new houses was often out of reach for young veterans. Post-war conditions placed two barriers in front of families trying to buy their first home: availability and cost. Veterans and their families often found it difficult, if not impossible, to find an adequate place to live. A letter published in the February 22, 1950 edition of the <u>North Town News</u> reflects the frustration of one veteran's family. While the writer blamed rent control, her issue seemed to be with the cost of new houses.

Opposite top: Indian Boundary Park lagoon with the Park Gables co-op apartments in the background.

Opposite bottom: Snapshot of children at the Indian Boundary Park lagoon in the 1940s.

Right top and bottom: Architecture typical of the 1950s building boom in West Ridge.

Sir:

I am writing a letter I have long put off on the subject of rent control. You cannot deny that the veterans are the worst sufferers because of this law. They are the last people to enter the housing market because they were called to war. My husband, myself and my daughter live in a miserable 2-room basement apartment and have lived here for five years. We are doing our best toward not keeping up the rest of the economy by not buying a car, by not buying a television set and by not even buying all the clothes we could. We're saving for the mythical reasonably priced home that undoubtedly doesn't exist. Meanwhile, we have a miserable life with our quarters even prohibiting any sort of social life. There are undoubtedly thousands of others like us. What effect has this on your economy or conscience?

Veteran's Wife

In response to the housing shortage, an unprecedented period of residential construction began in 1946. While new residential construction occurred in all parts of Chicago, it was especially dramatic on the city's Far North Side. Lots scattered throughout Rogers Park provided space for the construction of many buildings, while in West Ridge, large undeveloped areas and numerous lots were vacant and ready for hundreds of new houses and apartments.

In 1946, a local veteran was discharged from the army. With his wife, and their two sons, he returned to Chicago. In 1947, the family built a house on the 2800 block of Fitch Avenue, in West Ridge.

There weren't many places in Chicago where we felt Jewish people could buy a house. We liked the neighborhood and knew Jewish people lived there. Then we got lucky finding a lot and someone who would build a house we could afford.

Ilse Lewin

When the family moved into their new house, in October of 1947, there were seven vacant lots on the block. Within two years, new houses would be standing on six of the lots.

A preview of the population explosion appeared in 1946 when the Federal Government chose a field in the northwest section of West Ridge to build prefabricated houses as temporary housing for returning veterans and their families. The section, with small frame, rectangular houses, covered an area of approximately four square blocks and was located east of Washtenaw Avenue and south of Rogers School. By 1951, families living in the temporary housing had moved out, and the buildings were torn down in the mid-1950s.

Some examples of the housing construction boom in West Ridge and Rogers Park were described in the <u>North Town News</u>, the neighborhood newspaper:

Time Builders announced it would build 100 individual two-story Georgian homes in the northwest part of West Ridge, in an area bounded by Albany, Touhy, Kedzie and Sherwin. (3/19/50)

Twenty-eight new single-family houses and an apartment building were recently completed in West Ridge. (5/16/52)

The largest veteran's housing project in Chicago will be on a three-block area on Seeley, between Columbia and Albion. There will be thirty-seven buildings, each with four units. Veterans will be able to buy the four room units for $10,000, with $2,030 down and monthly payments of $70. (8/13/51)

Construction of ten new six-room town houses at Jarvis and Claremont was announced. (12/10/52)

Time Builders has constructed 350 homes in West Ridge in the last three years. (1/7/53)

Sixty-four new brick homes will be built by Roxbury Builders near Kedzie. (3/4/53)

Nine new buildings, with 275 apartments are going up in three West Ridge locations. (11/3/53)

Opposite: The clay pit area, c. 1950, on the east side of Kedzie between Pratt and Touhy. The Winston Towers condominium apartments were later built on this site. Photograph by Edward J. Taylor.

Construction continued throughout the 1950s. Chicago's Deputy Housing and Redevelopment Director announced that West Ridge led all other communities in home construction in 1957 with 802 new living units. A distant second that same year, was Rogers Park, which added 233 new units. West Ridge also surpassed all others in 1956 with 633 new units.

While the residential building boom tapered off in the 1960s, there was still one major undeveloped section in West Ridge, the area bounded by Sacramento, Pratt, Kedzie and Touhy. This eighty-acre piece of land was owned by the Illinois Brick Company, which had used it to dig up clay for bricks. During the 1940s, the clay was used up and the land was left with a gigantic sixty-five foot deep pit. In 1948, the Illinois Brick Company leased the land to the John Sexton Construction Company to fill in the clay pit and develop the area. It took the company *fifteen years* to complete the project.

In 1964, the Winston Muss Co. purchased fifty acres along the east side of Kedzie and began constructing five condominium apartment buildings. The project, called Winston Towers, added a total of 932 apartments to the neighborhood.

The building boom was not part of an organized plan, so the dramatic increases in construction and population stretched the infrastructure beyond its capacity. The new houses in the Deere Park area seemed to overtax the sewer system. After construction was completed, major rainstorms often resulted in flooded basements in the area. Soon, when there was a heavy storm, many families would form a line to hand up possessions stored in the basement. Basement flooding was a problem until a new sewer system was built in the 1960s. The increased traffic of heavy construction equipment accelerated the deterioration of many neighborhood streets, which had to be repaved. Also during this period, the city began paving gravel-covered alleys. This resulted in many residents receiving unexpected assessments from City Hall.

Although the residential building boom slowed in the early 1960s, the construction of new stores and businesses did not come to an end. The exploding population created many opportunities as new commercial areas appeared throughout both neighborhoods, and most of the vacant lots on Devon between Western and California were developed for commercial and residential use.

While West Ridge was dealing with the effects of new construction, Rogers Park was encountering the problems of an older neighborhood. In July 1959, Richard Dooley, chairman of the Rogers Park Development Commission, warned about signs of decay in the area. He mentioned many frame and stucco homes that were showing their age, impressive homes on Sheridan that had been converted to boarding houses and nursing homes, business areas that were struggling financially, and an abundance of billboards and dingy store fronts.

To address the problems, Dooley suggested a comprehensive plan, including financial support from the city, designation of Rogers Park as a "conservation area," which would force owners to repair their buildings, and rezoning to allow high-rise apartment buildings on Sheridan Road.

Changes were gradually implemented and Rogers Park held its reputation as one of the city's best neighborhoods.

New Residents

The building boom brought thousands of new families to the area. Many ethnic groups moved into Rogers Park during the 1950s and early 1960s A majority of the new residents were white, and many were Jewish.

On August 10, 1966, one hundred Rogers Park religious and community leaders publicly welcomed Negroes into the community. Within the next few months, ten black families moved into the area without incident, opening the door for peaceful integration. ***Chicago Tribune****, April 20, 1967*

In the post-war years, many Jews encountered both overt and subtle anti-Semitism. Jews felt they could live in only a few neighborhoods in Chicago. West Ridge had a Jewish presence so they felt welcome, and the unprecedented construction boom provided opportunities to purchase homes. As a result, the majority of the new West Ridge residents in the 1950s and 1960s were Jewish. By 1970, West Ridge had the largest Jewish population of any Chicago neighborhood.

The Jewish Community

The Rogers Park Jewish community began to develop as early as the 1910s when Congregation B'nai Zion and Temple Mizpah were first formed. In 1950, out of a total population of 62,252 in Rogers Park, 20,375 (approximately one-third) were Jewish with a concentration in the area bounded by Lake Michigan on the east, Devon on the south, Ashland on the west and Touhy on the north. During the next twenty years, the number of Jewish residents in the area continued to increase

Synagogues rapidly appeared in the area to meet the needs of the burgeoning Jewish population. The first, the North Boundary Temple, a Reform Jewish congregation, was organized in 1946, under the leadership of Rabbi Joseph Strauss. The congregation, which met at a hall at 6424 N. Western (currently the home of the *Rogers Park/West Ridge Historical Society)*, soon changed its name to Temple Menorah. By the end of the year, construction had started on the temple building at 2800 W. Sherwin at the corner of California. Several blocks south, at 2800 W. North Shore, an Orthodox Jewish congregation, K.I.N.S. of Rogers Park, was organized around 1949. A third synagogue, Ner Tamid, was started in 1935. This Conservative congregation was at 2754 W. Rosemont. New Jewish congregations continued to appear in West Ridge throughout the period.

Social Institutions

Jewish Community Centers (JCCs) addressed social, religious, and athletic needs of the Jewish community, and often provided social services, such as help for the elderly. The Rogers Park JCC was started in 1949 at 1222 Morse, and relocated to 7101 N. Greenview in 1955. To address the needs of the rapidly growing Jewish community in West Ridge, the Bernard Horwich JCC, at 3003 Touhy, was dedicated in 1960.

In 1951, High Ridge YMCA opened at 2400 Touhy. Many residents joined High Ridge,

Top: Breaking ground for the new High Ridge YMCA building at 2434 Touhy in 1952.

Bottom: High Ridge YMCA building in 1955, before the swimming pool was added. Chicago Historical Society, ICHi-25885; photograph by Martin J. Schmidt.

204 ROGERS SCHOOL 3B-3A. NOV. 1949.

302 ARMSTRONG SCHOOL 6B-5A.

Top left: Rogers School third grade class picture in November 1949.

Top right: Armstrong School fifth and sixth grade class picture in 1948.

Bottom: Rogers School original building prior to construction of two additions.

including a large number of Jewish families. High Ridge provided gym classes, basketball, children's activities and programs and recreational opportunities for adults, as well as "Camp A'Homa", a summer day camp. To support the "needs" of girls, "Teen 'Y' Charm" was presented. The class, geared to seventh and eighth grade girls, addressed, "...care of hair, skin, teeth and nails, posture, good grooming, etiquette, clothes and accessories, personality and poise."

Ten years after High Ridge opened, a unique pool was added to the building. The covered pool had sliding glass doors on two sides which, when opened in summer, created the feel of an outdoor pool.

Grade School Overcrowding

In the 1940s, there were eight public elementary schools (kindergarten through eighth grade) and several parochial schools located throughout Rogers Park and West Ridge. The schools in the area easily accommodated the students.

During the 1950s, the major challenge to the neighborhood schools was accommodating the overwhelming number of new children. The situation was more serious in West Ridge because of the unprecedented population explosion. At first, the schools addressed the problem by increasing class size. It soon became evident that additional steps were needed and most schools went to a double shift, with half the children attending school from 8 a.m. to noon, and the other half attending from noon to 4 p.m. While this doubled capacity, some schools were forced to send children in the upper grades to less crowded schools.

Shifts provided interim relief, but children lost an hour of school each day. Sending children to other schools involved bus rides at a time when most children walked to their grade schools. While schools were using different approaches to handle the overcrowding, principals and PTAs were pressuring the Chicago Board of Education to build additions as soon as possible. Additions to four area schools were completed in the early 1950s: Rogers (twelve classrooms), Boone (eight classrooms), Stone (four classrooms) and Clinton (twelve classrooms).

While the West Ridge schools were seriously affected by the population explosion, the impact on Rogers School was most dramatic. Built in 1937 in an area that was mostly prairie, Rogers, one of the smallest schools in Chicago, had eleven classrooms, a teachers' lounge and a small library. The building had no gym, lunchroom or auditorium. The school's enrollment in 1937 was 258. Enrollment rose to 508 in 1950, 1000 in 1952 and exceeded 1500 by the middle of the decade.

Rogers School, led by its principal, Dr. Benjamin Elkin, addressed the challenge of enrollment overload. In 1950, children in grades one through five attended school in shifts. Sixth grade through eighth grade had full school days but were in rooms with as many as three different grade levels.

In 1951, seventh and eighth grades were sent to classrooms at Jamieson School. The remaining students attended school on shifts. With some children in classrooms at Jamieson and the others attending in shifts, there was no opportunity to get all the students together. Even if the opportunity arose, the school did not have an assembly hall. Dr. Elkin was concerned that conditions could destroy school spirit. In order to improve morale among the students, Dr. Elkin instituted a series of tape-recorded programs. Several times during the year, each class recorded a brief program. The contributions were transferred to a single tape and played in each class. Rogers School received a commendation from the School Broadcasters Conference for the recorded programs.

In 1952, Rogers' first addition was completed, adding twelve classrooms and a new library. A branch was built six blocks from Rogers, at Touhy and Sacramento. The branch added six new classrooms, in three "cottage-type" bungalows, for kindergarten and primary grade children in the western end of the Rogers and Boone school districts.

The building addition and annex more than doubled the school's capacity, and the school remained on shifts, but Rogers was still unable to keep up with the continuing increase in students. In January 1953, part of the 6A class found itself assigned to the "floating division," under the strict control of Bertha McDaniel, a teacher who took discipline to the next level. Each morning, the members of the floating division reported to the teachers' lounge where they left their "wraps" (teacher talk for hats and coats). They lined up, carrying their school supplies in cigar boxes, and trudged to a room temporarily vacated by students who were at gym, home mechanics or the library. Mrs. McDaniel would teach a subject until regular occupants of the room returned. Then the floating division packed up and moved to the next temporary location. Fortunately, the floating division lasted only one semester.

Marv Brooderson started his teaching career in 1952 at William Penn School, on the

South Side of Chicago. In January of 1955, he transferred to Rogers School where he taught fifth and sixth grade. As of 2000, Mr. Brooderson, age 70, is the Assistant Principal at Rogers. During the 1950s, the Board of Education designated a class size of 40 children. In reality, the number was usually higher.

> *"I got up to 46 or 48, and that was the average class size in this school when I got here…The neighborhood around the school was like the Ivory Soap commercial, 99 and 44/100 % Jewish."*
> **Marv Brooderson, Rogers School Assistant Principal**

In 1958, a new school, Stephen Decatur, at 7030 N. Sacramento, replaced the Rogers annex. Decatur took students in kindergarten through fourth grade from the western section of the Rogers and Boone districts. There were now three schools to handle the neighborhood children.

In February of 1959, Decatur became a kindergarten through sixth grade school. In the 1960s, the population explosion slowed down and school enrollments leveled out. West Ridge schools had survived the crisis.

High School Overcrowding

Most public school students from Rogers Park and West Ridge attended Sullivan High School. Many students from Boone and Clinton found themselves attending Senn High School in the adjoining Edgewater community. Catholic schools provided additional options. St. George, a high school for boys, was located in the suburb of Evanston, only three blocks

north of Howard and just east of Ridge. St. Scholastica Academy, a high school for girls, was at 7416 N. Ridge.

Sullivan High School, a three-story red brick building, built in 1926, was surrounded by houses and older apartment buildings. The school handled the dramatic rise in enrollment during the 1950s by increasing class size and adding a tenth period. Some relief came in 1959 with the opening of Mather High School, but overcrowding was still a problem. During the early 1960s, up to six classrooms in Kilmer Elementary School were used by Sullivan for freshman classes.

In 1955, St. Scholastica began raising funds to expand its facilities. Construction of an addition started in 1956 and was completed in 1958. In addition to two new classrooms, the school added an auditorium, a lecture hall, a school office, an art department, a business department, and a music department with practice rooms and a choral room.

The Korean "War"

In June of 1950, North Korea invaded South Korea. The United Nations Security Council called for UN members to supply armed forces to restore peace in the area. By the end of June, President Truman had ordered Air Force, Navy and Army personnel to Korea to support the UN effort. Five years after the end of World War II, the United States was again at war, except it wasn't officially a war -- it was called a "police action," and it wasn't even our action -- the United States was supporting the United Nations.

At first, the Federal Government seemed to downplay the impact of the Korean con-

flict. In Rogers Park and West Ridge, as in other neighborhoods across the country, there was little concern about what was happening in Korea. In August of 1950, a new Draft Board office opened in Rogers Park, at 1605 W. Devon, and the North Town News sent a reporter to cover the event. The article that appeared in the paper emphasized décor and furnishings of the facility without any mention of the impact of the draft on families in the neighborhoods.

Soon residents began to take the threat of the Korean conflict more seriously as increasing numbers of men from the area were drafted or enlisted in the armed forces. By October, every issue of the North Town News included articles about men from the neighborhoods who were serving in Korea.

> *Pfc. J. A. Thinnes (7418 N. Western) is missing in action (1/10/51)*
>
> *Lt. Robert Meyer (6230 N. Rockwell) has been awarded two Gold Stars. The Marine pilot has completed 60 combat missions (8/15/51)*
>
> *Cpl. Robert Jones (2326 W. Estes) was wounded in the leg (8/27/52)*
>
> *Cpl. Allan Newman Jr. (6418 N. Talman) was awarded a Purple Heart (6/12/53)*
>
> *Capt. Robert Fink, a pilot, was shot down in Korea and presumably captured (6/17/53)*

While the spirit of the home front during the Korean War did not rival the total dedication of World War II, there was concern and support for the war effort. For example, on March 15, 1952, the Holy Name Society of St. Margaret Mary Church held a St. Patrick's Day party and proceeds from the party were used to send gifts to the sixty-four boys from the parish who were in the service.

In July of 1954, the Korean armistice was signed and the "police action" was over. The November 17, 1954 North Town News announced that the 750,000th GI to return from Korea was West Ridge resident Walter Seegren, who lived at 6215 N. Claremont.

The Battle Against Polio

The threat of polio (infantile paralysis) terrified Americans during the 1940s and the early 1950s. Pictures of polio wards, with dozens of people lying in iron lungs, appeared in newspapers and magazines. Neighborhood newspapers brought the disease to a personal level, and almost everyone knew of someone who had contracted the disease. The cause of polio was not known, but it was suspected that it was spread at swimming pools and in crowds during hot weather. In the late 1940s, the Chicago Park District converted its wading pools to sprinkler pools that did not retain water. The wading pool at Indian Boundary Park was converted during this period. Also, many swimming pools and summer camps throughout the area were closed.

_____

The memory of a young mother of two who died of infantile paralysis has been honored in a fashion that will help bring re-

*lief to others stricken with the disease. The young mother was Diane M. Brittain, who died Aug. 2, 1952. In her memory an iron lung was presented to Cook County chapter of National Infantile Paralysis recently in Wesley Memorial Hospital. The respirator was a gift of the Diane M Brittain Polio Foundation, of which Mrs. Brittain's husband, Gilbert H., 2640 Greenleaf, is president. A total of $2,500 to purchase the lung was raised by members of the foundation...**North Town News, June 23, 1954***

_____

In 1952, Jonas Salk developed an injectable vaccine for infantile paralysis. The vaccine was distributed nationally in 1954. In the spring of 1955, teams of doctors and nurses began providing free inoculations to first and second grade students in Chicago's public, parochial and private schools. On April 27, the children of St. Margaret Mary School, 7318 N. Oakley, became the first in the area to be inoculated. Children in the north side's public schools began receiving the vaccine on May 2. After the first and second graders were inoculated, elementary school children in other grades, and high school students, received the vaccine.

The effectiveness of the new vaccine was soon evident. In 1955, thirty-six new cases of polio were reported on the North Side. During the first six months of 1956, only one new case of polio was reported in the area. In 1960, the Salk vaccine was replaced by a vaccine developed by Albert Sabin. The Sabin Vaccine, delivered on sugar cubes, became an obvious preference of children instead of the Salk inoculation.

No Dancing Here

In the early 1950s, New York disc jockey Alan Freed angered parents, police, politicians and religious leaders as he introduced his white teenage audiences to rock and roll, including music of black artists. Freed was continuously attacked and harassed for playing "immoral" music that, his critics claimed, would drive innocent teens to delinquency, if not savage frenzy. A minor skirmish over rock and roll occurred in Rogers Park in March of 1957 when two local disc jockeys, Reed Farrell and "Spider" Webb, applied for a license to present Friday night record hops for teens at the Capri Ballroom, 1550 W. Devon.

1,850 concerned residents quickly signed a petition opposing the dances and Rogers Park Police Captain Ralph Petacque recommended that the license be denied. Residents opposed to the dances were concerned about the "rock and roll nature of the dances," a "lack of organized sponsorship and supervision," and the ever-popular, "the dances can bring juvenile delinquency into the neighborhood."

_____

My thirteen-year-old daughter shouldn't dance with nineteen-year-old boys.
A Concerned Mother

_____

We are operating the dances in an effort to avert juvenile delinquency by giving teen-agers some place to have good clean fun outside of school and church or temple.
Reed Farrell and "Spider" Webb

_____

Big Business

Rogers Park and West Ridge were residential, rather than industrial, neighborhoods, but two major companies, A. C. Nielsen Company and S & C Electric Company were located in Rogers Park.

The A. C. Nielsen Company was founded by Arthur C. Nielsen, Sr. and located at 2101 Howard from 1935 to 1972. Nielsen provided statistical reports and analysis to companies buying their service. The company's first business activity involved sending employees to grocery and drug stores to collect sales figures. Statisticians studied the data and prepared market reports which were among the first market research studies. Next, the company began measuring the size and composition of the audiences of radio shows, and later television shows. With the exploding popularity of television in the 1950s, the "Nielsen ratings" became a household name.

S & C Electric Company manufactures switching equipment and fuses used in power lines across the country. The company is run by John Conrad, son of Nicholas Conrad, co-founder of Schweitzer and Conrad. S & C, located at 6601 N Ridge, continues to be a presence in Rogers Park.

Top: Nicholas Conrad, one of the original owners of S&C Electric Company, with shovel, participates in the ceremonial groundbreaking at 6601 N. Ridge.

Bottom: S&C Electric Company begins construction on their first building in 1949 on their newly acquired property between 6545 and 6615 N. Ridge.

Devon - Heart of the Neighborhoods

In the '40s, '50s and '60s, next to downtown, Devon was the nicest street in the city. It was always clean. The stores were very nice and there were some excellent restaurants. People could buy almost everything they needed on Devon.
Ross Filecia

Devon was the most important and vibrant street in the area. It was a business section, a recreational area and a section of the community that provided neighborhood residents with strong, positive memories. The street had corner grocery stores and supermarkets, small clothing stores and department stores, snack shops and restaurants, and an array of stores and businesses to meet virtually every need. Recreation opportunities were provided by four movie theaters, two bowling alleys, a ballroom and, for those unsure of their skills, two dance studios.

Cook County Federal Saving started the period at 2326 W. Devon. In 1953, a large colonial building with chimes and a clock was constructed at Devon and Fairfield. This new home of Cook County Federal became a hallmark of Devon.

The street had several different personalities. The east end started at Sheridan Road, near Lake Michigan, Loyola University, Mundelein College and the Granada, a large, opulent art deco theater. The Granada was "a place to be" on a Friday or Saturday night. From Sheridan to Ridge, Devon was filled with small businesses, stores and restaurants. On the south side of Devon, west of Ridge, was Angel Guardian church and orphanage. The rest of the area between Ridge and Western was occupied with small businesses, stores and restaurants.

From Western to Mozart, Devon was a street of upscale stores, specialty shops, restaurants, grocery stores and variety stores, occasionally separated by vacant lots. The western section, from Mozart to Kedzie, was sparsely developed.

Shopping on Devon, especially the upscale area west of Western, was an important part of life in the neighborhoods. Prior to the twice a year "Dollar Days", which started in the 1930s, the North Town News printed front-page articles with large headlines enthusiastically announcing the upcoming sale. A major article followed each Dollar Days, recapping the *thrilling* event.

Dollar Day sales expanded throughout the neighborhoods. A Rogers Park Dollar Days was introduced in 1958. Howard Street merchants, as well as smaller shopping areas such as the Howard and Western shopping center, and California and Touhy, began their own Dollar Day events.

In 1950, the streetcar tracks on Devon, between Western and California, were torn out and the street was repaved. This closed the street to traffic for sixty days. Both business owners and shoppers were concerned about lack of access to the stores. The Nortown Chamber of Commerce sponsored a "Business As Usual" campaign, with parking on adjoining streets, "lucky shoppers," promotions and treasure hunts.

The reopening of Devon was celebrated on September 22 with a ceremony led by television personality Ernie Simon (the "Curbstone Cutup"), a parade, a host of politicians, including Mayor Martin Kennelly, and radio and television personalities. The celebration also included a "largest family contest" (won by Mr. and Mrs. H. C. Meyer and their "fourteen blessings"), an "oldest resident contest" and, to top off the festivities, a beauty contest, "Miss Modernized Devon."

Some of the more significant early businesses in the eight-block area from Western to Mozart were:

Crawford, a department Store at 2509 W. Devon, which alternately called itself "your fashion store" and "your friendly store." The North Town News often printed "news" items about the store. In the March 7, 1951 edition, Crawford announced that Mrs. Alline Winter had graduated, with the highest grades, from the Gossard School of Corsetry. The store proudly announced, *"This brings the number of graduate corsetiers at Crawford's to six."* An equally exciting item appeared on April 11, 1951, when it was announced that, *"The soft strains of Muzak melodies will waft through the local store...Neighbors can shop with the added charm of a musical background."*

Abrams, 2425 W. Devon, another department store, was the favorite place for children to buy shoes. The store carried Red Goose Shoes. From exposure to radio and television commercials, most young children believed that "Half the fun of having feet is wearing Red Goose shoes." Also, the children's shoe department had a fluoroscope, a device that provided an

Top: The 2700 block of Devon Avenue looking west in 1958. The colonial style building was the new location of Cook County Federal Savings. Slenderella was a 1950's weight-loss business. Chicago Historical Society, ICHi-25989; Photograph by Glenn Dahlby.

Bottom: Devon Avenue looking east toward Artesian in 1958. Hillman's was the major food store in the area during the 1950s. Chicago Historical Society, ICHi-25864; Photograph by Glenn Dahlby.

Top: Southwest corner of Devon and Western in the 1950s.

Bottom: The 1300 block of Devon Avenue looking west from Magnolia in 1962. Chicago Historical Society, ICHi-25855; Photograph by Glenn Dahlby.

x-ray view of a child's feet. The fluoroscope was a wildly popular device. It provided children with a great view of their feet and answered a parent's key question, "Is there some room for growth?"

Kenmac Radio Center, originally at 6348 N. Western, later at 2455 Devon, sold radios, televisions, records and appliances. Big name local entertainers, including WIND disc jockey Eddie Hubbard, recording artist and WGN radio personality Two-Ton Baker ("the Music Maker"), jazz great Art Van Damme, and vocalist Bonnie Baker appeared at the store's grand opening on February 11, 1950. Kenmac quickly became the major record store in the area due to its great selection of records, and booths, which enabled customers to listen to records. A few years later, Kenmac became primarily a record store. Few teens traveled Devon without a stop at Kenmac.

Manzelmann, 2749 W. Devon, was originally a hardware store. Through the years it added gifts, toys, lamps and furniture and became a predecessor of today's super stores. Its location encouraged businesses to open in the area west of California. In 1956, Manzelmann moved one block west to a larger location.

Woolworth's, which opened at 2405 W. Devon in 1950, was a classic '50s "dime store" with an amazing array of merchandise, a lunch counter, a pet section (goldfish and small turtles), and vending machines. The store was always filled with housewives and virtually every child touring Devon stopped at Woolworth's.

Hobbymodels opened in 1945 at 6337 N. Claremont. In 1948, the store moved to 6411 N. Western and, in 1959, it moved again, to 2358 W. Devon. At a time when the roles and interests of boys and girls were strictly defined, Hobbymodels was a powerful experience for most boys. An incredible collection of car, plane and ship model kits at every level of complexity filled the store, and completed models were everywhere. Toy soldiers were for sale and shown in realistic displays. Sports equipment was also available, and the store always had a supply of "Clinchers," the official sixteen-inch softball.

Ross Barber Shop opened in September of 1945, at 2639 W. Devon, and moved to its current location, 2813 W. Devon, in 1987. Ross Filecia's son, Joe, joined him in 1966 and, as of 2000, the father-son team was still running the shop. The owner of the shop remembered that, in the '40s and '50s, the shop was filled with boys virtually every day after school. They were there to choose one of the three parent approved, haircuts: a crew cut, a flat top or a "regular hair cut". Most boys came with instructions from their mothers and faced the embarrassment of a return visit with a parent if the barber did not receive the correct information.

By the late 1950s, boys were emulating the long, greasy look of the young, popular movie and singing stars. Pompadours seemed to rise in direct proportion to increases in the height of the automobile tail fins. The arrival of the Beatles in 1964 changed barbering, and introduced new hairstyles, which replaced the parent-favored "regular hair cut".

In 1955, when I was a seventh grader in Armstrong School, I had this routine. Just about every Saturday morning I did this walk around Devon My first stop was always Kenmac. I went into a booth and listened to records until lunchtime, or until Mac (one of the owners) pointed out that there were people waiting for a booth. I always stopped at Woolworth's for lunch. Fifteen-cent hot dog, five-cent root beer. No tax. The best lunch in the world. Before leaving Woolworth's I'd look at the makeup. Sometimes I'd put a dime in a machine and stamp out a message on a round metal disc... I walked west on Devon. I stopped in at several clothing stores, not the real expensive ones. I usually didn't have enough money to buy anything. At Mozart, I crossed the street and headed back to Western. Sometimes I'd stop at Neisners, a dime store. They had these homemade ice cream sandwiches. They'd cut a square of neapolitan ice cream and place it between two wafers... Walking on Devon, it was just a Jewish world. Everyone was Jewish, the storeowners, the delis. You always ran into people you knew. It was like your neighborhood.
Judith Loberg Rock

New stores were continuously opening on Devon. Seymour Paisin Dress Shop, an upscale store, opened in April of 1951, at 2641 W. Devon. The <u>North Town News</u> advised its readers that the store had "attractive dressing booths." WGN radio personality Wally Phillips made the store a household name by giving many of his callers "a designer scarf from Seymour Paisin." On the other end of the luxury spectrum, in September of 1953, a Robert Hall men's clothing store opened at 2935 W. Devon. The store promised that, "Robert Hall does not spend money on expensive fronts, fancy fixtures and high rent locations -- all of which add to selling costs."

Randl's "Florida Style Restaurant" was on the southwest corner of California and Devon. The popular delicatessen and restaurant was the scene of a minor controversy. On weekend evenings, teens hung out in front of Randl's, generating another "juvenile delinquency" alert, as many residents were convinced that any group of two or more teens standing in front of a store were juvenile delinquents.

Another popular restaurant, Kofields, "The Northside's Most Beautiful Restaurant-Snack Shop," was on the northwest corner of California and Devon. Though it was across the street from Randl's, Kofields did not attract the dreaded "loitering teens." Western and Devon had similar restaurant-delicatessens. In the early 1960s, Nathans was on the southwest corner (later occupied by La Petite Restaurant) and Peter Pan Restaurant was across the street. Pekin House, east of Western, was a favorite for fans of Chinese food, and was mentioned in any debate about "the greatest egg rolls."

Right: Kofield's Restaurant, 2758 W. Devon, on northeast corner at California in 1958. Chicago Historical Society, ICHi-25859; Photograph by Glenn Dahlby.

I loved going to Devon. When I was about ten, I went there every Saturday with my best friend, Allan Rosenberg. I think it was 1963. We always stopped at this little candy store, and bought candy for the show. Then we went to the Nortown for the matinee. After the show, we cut through the Western Ave. entrance to Woolworth's and looked at the goldfish and the small turtles. We left Woolworth's and walked along the south side of Devon to California, crossed the street, and stopped at Gigio's, a small pizza restaurant, for a "slice to go." Our final stop was Neisners. They had this machine. You put a nickel in it and shot twenty bee bees at small plastic outlaws. The whole day cost each of us less than two dollars. **Jeff Hecht**

Howard Street

Bethesda, one of the neighborhood's two hospitals (the other was Doctors Hospital on Clark) was on Howard, just west of Western. East of Ridge was the A. C. Nielsen Company headquarters, and just west of Ridge was a neighborhood institution, The Fish Keg, at 2233 W. Howard. For almost fifty years, people have visited the small store for fried and fresh shrimp. The area east of Clark was densely developed. In addition to the Howard Street elevated train station, "modernized" in 1963, there were many small shops, a supermarket and restaurants. People from the North Side of Chicago and Evanston took advantage of two movie palaces, the Howard Theatre, which was east of the station, and the

Opposite top: A view of Howard Street looking east from the elevated platform, c. 1950.

Opposite bottom: The Howard elevated station at Howard and Hermitage, c. 1950.

Right: Howard looking east from Clark in 1955. The Norshore Theatre was featuring "Lady and the Tramp."

Left: The Norshore Theatre at 1749 W. Howard in 1960, shortly before it was razed.

Opposite top: Bethesda Hospital at 2451 W. Howard in 1960. Chicago Historical Society, ICHi-25865; Photograph by Tom H. Long.

Opposite bottom: Site of the Howard-Western Shopping Center before the start of construction in the late 1950s.

Norshore Theatre, located between the Howard train station and Clark. Howard Bowl was near the Norshore.

Restaurants in the eastern area included Talbott's Bar-B-Q on Paulina Street, and the Limehouse, Hoe Hoe, and Papa Milano's on Howard. East of the Howard train station was Pan Dee's, a small snack shop and ice cream parlor. One of Pan Dee's specialties was a sundae with twenty-four scoops of ice cream, syrup, nuts and whipped cream. Recognition was given to anyone who could finish the gigantic dish. Few were up to the challenge, but one afternoon in the mid 1950s, Mike Menaker, a North Side teenager with frightening metabolism, cheered on by a small but enthusiastic audience, joined the select group that had triumphed over the giant Pan Dee's sundae. Mike was awarded a certificate recognizing him as a *Sundae King*.

The "Howard Jubilee," an outdoor festival, was held in spring, at Howard and Ashland. As usual, the highlight was a beauty contest, the "Howard Jubilee Queen." In 1951, the event was held on March 9. The North Town News reported that, *"Mayor Martin H. Kennelly will crown the loveliest of an outstanding field of beauties… Some of the girls who will compete in the contest already have won titles too numerous to mention. They are the cream of the crop from the incubator of beauty - the North Side."*

Western Avenue

Running through the entire length of the city of Chicago, Western was the longest continuous street in the world. The section north of Peterson, called "Automobile Row," had several major new car dealers, including "Z"

Frank, "the world's largest Chevy Dealer", Nortown Olds, 5940 N. Western, People's Pontiac, 6116 N. Western and Bob Waller Buick, 6100 N. Western.

The Nortown Theater, 6320 Western, was just south of Devon. Restaurants on Western, between Rosemont and Howard, included Sally's Original Bar-B-Q, The Town Pump (opened in 1925), Black Angus, Miller's Steak House, Welcome Inn Pizzeria and Candlelite. These places seemed to reflect contemporary attitudes towards nutrition and dining.

Bowling was very popular, and many business, social and religious organizations had bowling leagues. There were three places to bowl on Western: Theater Bowl, at Western and Pratt, Markay Recreation Center, 7221 N. Western, the last bowling alley in the neighborhood to use pin boys, and Sunset Bowl and Health Club, 7304 N. Western.

Open all night on Fridays and Saturdays, Sunset Bowl was usually filled until 4 a.m. with teen-age boys recounting the adventures of their dates, as well as serious bowlers who competed against each other in high-stakes games.

Morse Avenue

The Morse elevated train station was the center of a small, but popular, commercial area. The most popular place was the legendary Ashkenaz Restaurant, a delicatessen and restaurant, which attracted hundreds of people each day.

Students from Sullivan High School would go to Morse for an alternative to the "fine" school cafeteria cuisine. Long lines at Ashkenaz usually caused Sullivanites to visit one of the other eating establishments in the

area. Kerr's Hamburgers, 1425 Morse, was across the street from Ashkenaz. The owner spent a great deal of time protecting his parking lot from intrusion by Ashkenaz patrons. Another option was Rocky's Luncheonette, 1417 Morse, which served such eclectic dishes as sweet and sour spaghetti. On the same block was Froikens's Knishery, where patrons carried out hot knish or a piece of kishke.

A Jewel Food Store opened on the 1400 block of Morse across from Ashkenaz. There was also a Davidson's Bakery and Morry's Men's Store located next to Ashkenaz, and the Coed movie theater, just east of the El station. Caswell's Drug Store, at Ashland and Morse, was a neighborhood institution.

Caswell's was really a store for everyone. The kids could buy candy, gum and baseball cards. It was the place where I bought school supplies each year, and Mr. Caswell would always save an empty cigar box for my school supplies. Adults bought their newspapers, cigarettes and cigars there.
Neal Samors

Sullivan High School

Sullivan High School, 6631 N. Bosworth, was built in 1926. During its first few years, it was a junior high school. Neighborhood children attended Sullivan for two years and then completed high school at Senn. After a few years, it became a four-year high school.

During most of this period, Sullivan excelled in academics; the number of scholarships achieved by some classes exceeded the number of graduates. Virtually everyone who

attended Sullivan remembers the large number of truly excellent teachers.

The boys' gym teachers were another matter. One gym session a week was supposed to be devoted to "Health" (whatever that was). Teaching this challenging subject usually involved taking a group of boys to a classroom, passing out some old Life magazines, and instructing the students to, *"Find an article about health and read it."*

Sullivan's "campus" was less than impressive. There were three gravel-covered yards that made outdoor gym classes a negative experience. The school also had a swimming pool; girls had to swim in dreaded *tank suits,* which started up where they belonged, but drooped as they got wet. Boys swam *au natural,* which meant they had little concern about swimwear. There are few fond memories of the swimming program.

Students rarely cut school during this time, due to the efforts of attendance counselors who were able to bring the most hardened would-be delinquents to tears. Miss O'Connell occupied this role for several years.

One of Sullivan's traditions, a monthly Friday night dance sponsored by the "Social Center," was launched on February 6, 1953. The first dance, *Moon Over Miami,* was a trial to determine student support. Of course, there was a dress code.

No bobby sox, open shirts or shirtsleeves will abridge the formality of the occasion, in keeping with the Board of Education's regulations for the dances it sponsors at other high school centers. **North Town News, February 4, 1953**

Right: Students gather in front of Sullivan High School in 1948. Photograph by Wilming Hugh.

A new English course reflected changes in the neighborhood. Starting in September 1961, Sullivan added *English F,* a class devoted to, *"conversational English, idiomatic expressions, and language training for foreign-born students."*

During the '50s and '60s, Sullivan students found a new way of getting to and from school. Jerry's Bus Service was actually Jerry and his bus. Jerry created his own route and charged a nickel for each ride. The bus was always very crowded.

I didn't ride Jerry's bus the first two years because I thought it was only for the popular kids. Then I started riding it when I was a junior. It was great.
Judith Loberg Rock

The Beaches

The Rogers Park beaches played many roles in the life of the community. Touhy Beach reflected the influence of a Chicago legend, beach director Sam Leone, who arrived in 1925 and remained until his death in 1965. Leone initiated a Junior Lifeguard program, which provided lifeguard training, sports and recreational activities to thousands of children. In 1970, the first girls joined the junior lifeguard program.

On summer weekends, the beaches were a place for family outings, while warm evenings found the sand crowded with people looking for relief from the heat.

During the week, the beaches, especially Morse Avenue, were covered with blankets occupied by teens who were there to work on their tans, talk and laugh with friends and, just possibly, meet that *special someone.* Also, boys played cards and softball.

Right: U.S. Coast Guard Life-Saving Boathouse at Touhy Beach in April of 1950.

Bottom: An early spring view of Touhy Beach in April 1950.

WJJD, a "Top Forty" radio station, was the only game in town in the '50s, and all the portable radios were tuned to the station, which could clearly be heard anywhere on the beach. *"And now, let's spin the number three song, Jimmy Rogers' 'Secretly!' "* In the '60s, WLS became the beach-dwelling teens' favorite radio station.

Weekend evenings brought still another group to the beach. Teenage couples parked in cars near the beach, listening to WCFL's Sid McCoy play Frank Sinatra music and soft jazz. Some walked along the sand or out on Farwell Pier, possibly the most romantic spot in the area.

Sports

It's impossible to think about sports during this period without recognizing the role of Mel Thillens. Thillens Stadium (also known as North Town Currency Exchange Stadium) located at Devon and Kedzie, along the west end of West Ridge, was a place to play and watch baseball and softball games. Novelty attractions appearing at the stadium included "The King and His Court" (a four-man softball team that took on, and usually defeated, all challengers), "The Queen and Her Court" and "Donkey Softball" (a self-descriptive name for a bizarre type of sports entertainment).

Sixteen-inch softball and men's and women's fast-pitch softball leagues played on Thillens two diamonds on a regular basis. In 1950, Mel Thillens introduced Little League baseball to the neighborhoods. He was unable to negotiate an agreement with the Little League organization so, in 1951, he started his own program, *Boys' Major League.* More than 500 boys, ages nine to twelve, tried out for one of the 140 spots on one of the four teams that would make up

Left: Thillens ball players pose in front of the grand prize automobile in a fund raising raffle at 2525 W. Touhy in the early 1950s.

Bottom: "The White Sox", a team in the Thillens Boys Major League in 1953.

Left: A member of Thillens Boys Major League is coached in 1963.

the new league. The league was launched on June 2, 1951, with a parade and festival. This was one of the few neighborhood events not capped off with a beauty contest.

The *Boys' Major League* eventually grew to 1,000 boys, the maximum the facility could handle. Mel Thillens encouraged the formation of other leagues so every boy in the neighborhoods would have a chance to make a team.

Sixteen-inch softball was "Chicago's game," invented in the city and played almost exclusively in the Chicago area until the '70s. In league play, each game started with a new, hard Clincher softball. No gloves were allowed, and men who played the game for any length of time usually had an assortment of fingers that were gnarled and pointed in unusual directions.

In the 1950s and '60s, every park in the neighborhoods with ball fields had a softball league, including Loyola Park, Leone Park, Touhy Park and Rogers School Park. As the popularity of the game grew, the number of leagues also grew. Mather Park, located on Peterson, in front of Mather High School, had league play Monday through Thursday evenings and Sunday morning. The Mather "A League" was the most competitive in the area.

Women joined the softball frenzy in the late '60s as women's leagues were started at several parks. Women played according to the rules of the "sixteen-inch" game, but used a fourteen-inch ball.

In the fall, touch and flag football leagues appeared in parks throughout the area, and High Ridge YMCA started a Pop Warner football team, the Chargers, that won several championships.

Children were able to adapt a game to virtually any surrounding using whatever equipment was available. Every side street, alley, vacant lot and schoolyard was a potential sports arena. There was "pinners" (throwing a rubber ball against the front stairs hard enough so the other players couldn't catch it), line ball in any alley, and softball almost anywhere.

Street football occupied almost every boy's attention in fall *"Fake to the right in front of the green Ford and I'll throw it to you as you cut towards Mr. Garfinkle's lawn."*

Legends and Traditions

Ashkenaz Restaurant and Delicatessen moved from the West Side of Chicago to 1432 W. Morse in 1937, and soon became immensely popular. The deli counter was always busy and there were long lines of eager diners at mealtime. Located in Rogers Park, near the Morse elevated train station, Ashkenaz attracted families for dinner, couples for late evening snacks, housewives and students from Sullivan High for lunch. Sunday brunch was a community event for older members of the Rogers Park Jewish Community.

At its busiest, Ashkenaz sold a half-ton of corned beef a month. In 1953 rumors that Ashkenaz was going to be sold passed around the neighborhood. In March, owners Hy Kalmin and Sam Ashkenaz placed an ad in the neighborhood newspaper reassuring their customers that "these rumors are unfounded. At no time have we contemplated nor been approached on the purchase of our establishment."

To the relief of its customers, Ashkenaz remained on Morse until the 1970s, when the area's declining Jewish population became a factor in the owners' decision to close the Morse Avenue landmark.

Field School had a tradition that made Halloween memorable. Each year, the children came to school in Halloween costumes and received free taffy apples from the Affy Tapple Company on Clark, north of Estes. Also, the costumed children paraded along Clark and then east on Morse. Students from the school were picked to decorate store windows on Morse and along Clark.

Devon was a favorite place to "trick-or-treat." Some fifty-year-old veterans of the ritual still remember getting "great stuff," including wooden yardsticks from a paint store.

In the '50s and '60s, Christian and Jewish students at Sullivan would decorate a Christmas tree and the school choir would sing Christmas and Hanukkah songs. Most of the public elementary schools in the area had similar celebrations for these two winter holidays.

Armstrong School had two memorable traditions, one more favorable than the other. Every June, near the end of the school year, Armstrong had "Field Day." The day started with parents and children eating a hot dog lunch. Soft drinks, cotton candy, popcorn and snow cones were available. At 1 p.m. sharp, the events started: races, volleyball and softball games. The events were strictly scheduled and ribbons were awarded.

The regimented nature of Armstrong created an atmosphere that was not as warmly remembered as Field Day. The school had a large force of monitors. Each morning, the students marched into the school. A monitor stationed at each landing would stop the students and repeat the same message: *"Walk up the stairs very slowly and quietly, lift your feet and keep your voices down."*

Years after leaving Armstrong, former students still remember the message they heard a dozen times every day.

Square Dancing had a stunning level of popularity in the 1950s. Virtually every organization, including PTAs, civic groups, and charities had one or more square dances. The Rogers School PTA had an annual barn dance, due in large part to the fact that school principal Benjamin Elkin fancied himself a square dance "caller." Alternatives to square dancing included such "legendary" acts as the Adairs Accordianettes.

The End of an Era

This period started with the end of a world war that received almost total support from the home front and ended as the United States became increasingly involved in a "limited war" in Vietnam, and home front reactions ranged from support to aggressive opposition. In 1965, 190,000 U.S. troops were in Vietnam and 25,000 people gathered in Washington to protest the war.

The number of Americans in Vietnam, and the number of people protesting the war, increased each year. While there were few protests on the North Side, once again men from the neighborhood were participating in a war. By 1969, 484,000 Americans were serving in Vietnam. The war would be officially over in 1975.

The 1960s also ended with a shift in population. Many families, including a large number of Reform Jews, left the neighborhoods for the suburbs. They were replaced by minorities, Eastern Europeans and Orthodox Jews. Throughout the 1970s, Rogers Park and West Ridge remained dynamic and changing neighborhoods.

Opposite top: Passengers board a Chicago and Northwestern train at the Kenmore Station (formerly High Ridge) at Granville and Ridge in the mid 1950s. Photograph courtesy of John Kammacher.

Opposite bottom: A Western Avenue streetcar turns around at the Devon Avenue car barn on Clark north of Devon in the mid 1950s.

Above: The Granada Theatre from the Loyola elevated station in 1960. Photograph by Howard B. Anderson.

AFTERWORD:
YEARS OF TRANSITION
AND DIVERSITY

While sociologists debate whether Chicago has become the most segregated city in America, census statistics indicate that Rogers Park and West Ridge, two communities on the Far North Side, are becoming so diverse that they might be considered microcosms of the city of Chicago's ethnic makeup.

A short walk down Devon Avenue best illustrates this point, with ethnic groups represented from a broad spectrum, including Indian, Pakistani, Russian, Jewish, Greek, Mexican, Caribbean, Polish, Chinese, Korean, Thai, and Vietnamese, to name only some of the groups. Signs in shop windows boast of the many languages spoken and of the variety of ethnic foods, clothing and services available to area residents. The public acceptance and celebration of diversity in Rogers Park and West Ridge might account for the fact that so many different immigrant groups have selected the neighborhoods as their points of entry for their new lives in America. Rogers Park and West Ridge have gained reputations, perhaps internationally, as neighborhoods that are proud of their diversity and the role they play in the lives of newcomers.

Throughout their 170-year history, Rogers Park and West Ridge have often been entry points for new residents. These included Irish, English, Swedish, German and Luxembourger settlers who came to the Chicago area to build new homes, farms and businesses. In addition, there were German, Russian and Hungarian Jews who had emigrated to America and chose the neighborhoods as good places to live and work. In more recent years, Blacks and Hispanics sought stable neighborhoods to raise their families and seek good housing and educational opportunities. Currently, there is a cornucopia of residents from diverse homelands including Asia, the Middle East, Europe, the Caribbean, Latin America and Africa.

Today, Rogers Park and West Ridge still replicate the process that the entire city of Chicago has followed through its history -- immigrant groups coming to America and settling in large cities and their neighborhoods. Small enclaves within communities provided familiarity, comfort and support to immigrants as they established their new lives. As those families prospered, they, and their succeeding generations, would often

move to less dense, more residential areas, whether other sections of the cities or nearby suburbs. Since the 1920s and the housing boom in Rogers Park, and then the post-war years of the mid- to late 1940s, and the development of new houses and apartment buildings in West Ridge, immigrants have chosen these neighborhoods as preferred locations for settlement.

Rogers Park and West Ridge have also attracted more senior citizens and, for the past thirty years, there has been a focus on the construction of retirement, assisted living, and nursing homes for that segment of the population. Although there has been a concentration of such buildings along and near Sheridan Road in Rogers Park, there are also numerous facilities for seniors in West Ridge. This has added to the age diversity in both

neighborhoods. In recent years there has also been gentrification in the housing stock from Sheridan to Kedzie and from Devon to Howard.

Overall, the thousands of residents who have called Rogers Park and West Ridge their home over the years have continued to appreciate the same characteristics of the neighborhoods that attracted them in the first place. These included excellent housing, transportation, schools, tree-lined streets and parks, convenient shopping, a broad array of entertainment venues and a strong sense of community. The people who live and work in the neighborhoods today come from a very different ethnic, racial and religious mix than the first settlers. The residents in the earlier part of the twentieth century and those who lived here from 1940 through 1970 all share one thing in common. They recognize and celebrate

the diversity and the rich history of Chicago's Far North Side.

Rogers Park and West Ridge are in the midst of another long series of transition periods. It began when Philip Rogers arrived in the region in the 1830s, extended through the development, incorporation and annexation of the villages, and continues today as both neighborhoods seek to restructure themselves for the future. It is truly a period of diversity and transition.

Opposite: Aerial view of East Rogers Park c. 1980.

Top left: Rogers Park Community Council Planning Conference, 1986. Photograph by Martin J. Schmidt.

Top right: Devon Avenue, display of saris, 1985. Chicago Historical Society: ICHi-23827, photograph by John McCarthy.

SOURCES

Books and Pamphlets

Chamberlain, Everett. *Chicago and Its Suburbs*. Chicago: T. A. Hungerford & Co., 1874.

The Chicago Fact Book Consortium. *Local Community Fact Book, Chicago Metropolitan Area,* Based on the 1970 and 1980 Censuses. Chicago: Chicago Review Press, 1984.

Cole, Harry Ellsworth, Louise Phelps Kellogg (ed.). *Stagecoach and Tavern Tale of the Old Northwest*. Carbondale, IL: Southern Illinois University Press, 1997.

Cutler, Irving. *The Jews of Chicago: From Shtetl to Suburb*. Urbana, IL: University of Illinois Press, 1996.

Danks, Gail Welter. *The Rogers Park Community: A Study of Social Change, Community Groups, and Neighborhood Reputation*. Chicago: Loyola University Press, 1982.

Davis, James Leslie. *The Elevated System and the Growth of Northern Chicago*. Northwestern University Studies in Geography, no. 10. Evanston: Northwestern University Department of Geography, 1965.

Drury, John. *Old Chicago Houses*. NY: Bonanza Books, 1941.

The East Rogers Park Neighborhood History Project, Public History Program. *Reading*

Your Neighborhood: A History of East Rogers Park. Chicago: Loyola University, 1993.

Ebner, Michael H. *Creating Chicago's North Shore*. Chicago: University of Chicago Press, 1988.

Keating, Ann Durkin. *Building Chicago: Suburban Developers & the Creation of a Divided Metropolis*. Columbus, OH: Ohio State University Press, 1988.

Mayer, Harold M. and Wade, Richard C. *Chicago: Growth of a Metropolis* Chicago: University of Chicago Press, 1969.

Pacyga, Dominic A. and Skerrett, Ellen. *Chicago: City of Neighborhoods*. Chicago: Loyola University Press, 1986.

Prairie Passage: The Illinois and Michigan Canal Corridor. Urbana, IL: University of Illinois Press, 1998.

Zaltman, Mark A. *Suburban/Rural Conflicts in Late 19th Century Chicago: Political, Religious and Social Controversies on the North Shore*. San Francisco: International Scholars Publications, 1998.

Documents

Palmer, Vivien M. (ed.). *History of the Rogers Park Community, Chicago*. Prepared for The Chicago Historical Society and the Local Community Research Committee, University of Chicago, 1927.

Palmer, Vivien M. (ed.). *History of the West Rogers Park Community, Chicago*. Prepared for The Chicago Historical Society and the Local Community Research Committee, University of Chicago, 1927.

Newspapers and Journals

Chicago Daily News
Chicago Evening Post
Chicago History
Chicago Sun-Times
Chicago Tribune
Evanston Index, The
Historian, The
Howard News, The
Journal of Illinois History
Lerner News
Lincolnite, The
Loyola News
North Shore News
North Town News
Northside Sunday Citizen
Rogers Park Historical Society Newsletter
Rogers Park News
Rogers Park News Herald

INDEX

ILLUSTRATION INDEX

ACKNOWLEDGMENTS

A general debt of gratitude is owed to the late Jacqueline Morrell McNicol, to Mary Jo Behrendt Doyle and to Martin J. Schmidt for providing an early vision for, and a long-term devotion to, the development of a history of Rogers Park and West Ridge.

We want to express our thanks to Jackie for suggesting a sense of the scope of the book, to Mary Jo for her years of devotion to the Rogers Park/West Ridge Historical Society and a commitment to creating the book, and to Marty for providing Chicago, and the Society, with an outstanding photographic record of the city and of the neighborhoods over the years.

This illustrated history could not have been published without the dedicated efforts of the Steering Committee that made a commitment to the creation and completion of the book. That committee included Mary Jo Doyle, Martin Lewin, Neal Samors and Michael Williams.

Special thanks are also due to Arthur C. Nielsen, Jr. for his generous financial contribution. Without that support, this book could not have been published.

Susan Sosin, Marilou Kessler, Sally Kirkpatrick and Marcee Williams, all key participants in the book's completion provided editorial support. James Kirkpatrick worked tirelessly with the Steering Committee to assure that the book would be of a high quality.

David Marshall offered historical information related to the development of transportation and Sandra Stone did extensive research on the parks. Steve Rowe joined the team to help create the index for the book.

Thank to Mel Thillens, Jr. and Dorsi Thillens Finnegan for the photos pertaining to Thillens Stadium and related events.

Special thanks are also due to Russell Lewis of the Chicago Historical Society for providing assistance and guidance as the Steering Committee continued its process of selecting the best available photographs of the neighborhoods.

Finally, Kenan Heise of Chicago Historical Bookworks, provided important advice on marketing and publishing strategies, and wrote the Foreword to the book.

Many other members of the Rogers Park/West Ridge Historical Society have provided support and guidance during the several years that were devoted to the completion of this book. We want to especially recognize the work of Ellen Eslinger and Thomas Serb.

In addition there are a few very special people who provided encouragement throughout this project. They include John E. Arcand, Mary Borke, Mary Chidester, Pat Daly, Jackie Dupon, Cathy Keenan, Loren P. Kringle, Eleanor Mars, Mervyn Ruskow, Jeanette Statland and Joan Thiry.

There are others too numerous to mention who contributed to this book in direct and indirect ways, and to them and those noted above, our thanks.

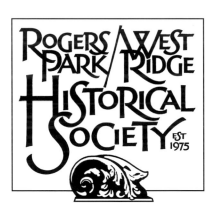